Demand Forecasting
for Managers

Demand Forecasting for Managers

Stephan Kolassa
Enno Siemsen

 BUSINESS EXPERT PRESS

First published in 2016 by
Business Expert Press, LLC
222 East 46th Street, New York, NY 10017
www.businessexpertpress.com

ISBN-13: 978-1-60649-502-5 (paperback)
ISBN-13: 978-1-60649-503-2 (e-book)

Business Expert Press Supply and Operations Management Collection

Collection ISSN: 2156-8189 (print)
Collection ISSN: 2156-8200 (electronic)

Cover and interior design by S4Carlisle Publishing Services
Private Ltd., Chennai, India

First edition: 2016

10 9 8 7 6 5 4 3 2 1

Printed in the United States of America.

Abstract

Most decisions and plans in a firm require a forecast. Not matching supply with demand can make or break any business, and that is why forecasting is so invaluable. Forecasting can appear as a frightening topic with many arcane equations to master. We therefore start out from the very basics and provide a nontechnical overview of common forecasting techniques as well as organizational aspects of creating a robust forecasting process. We also discuss how to measure forecast accuracy to hold people accountable and guide continuous improvement. This book does not require prior knowledge of higher mathematics, statistics, or operations research. It is designed to serve as a first introduction to the nonexpert, such as a manager overseeing a forecasting group, or an MBA student who needs to be familiar with the broad outlines of forecasting without specializing in it.

Keywords

forecasting; sales and operations planning; decision making; service levels; statistics thinking; choice under uncertainty; forecast accuracy; intermittent demand; forecasting competition; judgmental forecasting

Contents

Acknowledgments

We would like to thank Aris Syntetos, Len Tashman, Doug Thomas, Paul Goodwin, and Jordan Tong for their valuable feedback on earlier drafts of this manuscript.

Stephan Kolassa dedicates this book to I., S., & P. Enno Siemsen dedicates this book to O., T., & M.

PART I

Introduction

CHAPTER 1

Introduction

1.1. The Value of a Good Forecasting Process

It is common to become frustrated about forecasting. The necessary data is often dispersed throughout the organization. The algorithms used to analyze this data are often opaque. Those within the organization trained to understand the algorithms often do not understand the business, and those who breathe the business do not understand the algorithms. The actual forecast is then discussed in long and unproductive consensus meetings between diverse stakeholders with often conflicting incentives; in between, the forecast is often confused with goals, targets, and plans. The resulting consensus can be a political compromise that is far removed from any optimal use of information. These forecasts are in turn often ignored by decision makers, who instead come up with their own "guess" since they do not trust the forecast and the process that created it. Even if the forecasting process appears to work well, the actual, inherent demand uncertainty often creates numbers that are far away from the forecast. It is hard to maintain clarity in such a setting and not become frustrated by how hard it is to rely on forecasts.

Yet, what alternative do we have to preparing a forecast? The absence of a good forecasting process within an organization will only create worse parallel shadow processes. Every plan, after all, needs a forecast, whether that forecast is an actual number based on facts or just the gut feeling of a planner. Some companies can change their business model to a make-to-order system, eliminating the need to forecast demand and manufacture their products to stock, but this alternative model still requires ordering components and raw materials based on a forecast, as well as planning capacity and training the workforce according to an estimate of future demand. A central metric for every supply chain is how long it would take for all partners in the supply chain to move one unit—from the beginning to the end—into the market. This metric shows the total lead time in the supply chain. As long as customers are not willing to wait that long for a product, a supply chain cannot change to a complete make-to-order system. *Someone* in the supply chain will need to forecast and hold inventory. If that forecasting system does not work well, the resulting costs and disruptions will be felt throughout the supply chain.

One central tenet every manager involved in forecasting needs to accept is that there are no good or bad forecasts. There are only good or bad ways of creating or using forecasts. Forecasts should contain all the relevant information that is available to the organization and its supply chain about the market. Information is everything that reduces uncertainty. If a forecast is far away from the actual demand, but the process that generated the forecast made effective use of all available information, the organization simply had bad luck. Conversely, if a forecast is spot on, but the process that created it neglected important information, the organization was lucky but should consider improving their forecasting process. Bad forecasts in this sense can only be the result of bad forecasting processes. As with decision making under uncertainty in general, one should not question the quality of the decision or forecast itself given the actual outcome; one should only question the process that led to this decision or forecast. Betting money in roulette on the number 20 does not become a bad choice just because a different number is rolled—and neither does it become a better choice if the ball happens to actually land on the 20!

Different time series are more or less predictable, and if a series has a lot of unexplainable variation, there is a limit to how well it can be forecast. Figure 1.1 offers an example of two time series that are very different in terms of their forecastability. Importantly, while a good forecasting process will make time series more predictable by explaining some variation in the series, there are limits to the inherent predictability of such series. Repeated inaccurate forecasts can be a sign of a bad forecasting process, but they may also simply be a result of excessive noise in the underlying demand. The inherent forecastability of the series should thus be taken into account when judging the quality of a forecasting process. In this sense, a good forecasting process is not necessarily a process that makes a time series perfectly predictable but a process that improves the

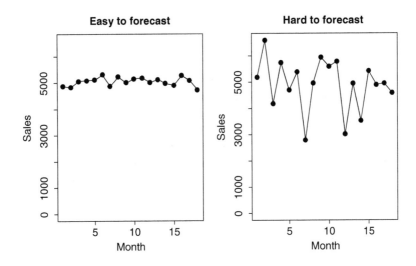

Figure 1.1 Easy- and hard-to-forecast time series

predictability of a series compared to simple forecasting methods.[1] We will discuss the concept of forecastability in more detail in Chapter 4.

From this perspective, one may be surprised to see how many organizations still exclusively rely on the use of point forecasts. A point forecast is a single number—an estimate of what an unknown quantity will most likely be. It is, however, highly unlikely that the actual number will be exactly equal to the point forecast. Thus, one always needs to think about and deal with the remaining uncertainty in the forecast. Ideally, one should conceptualize a forecast as a probability distribution. That distribution can have a center, which is usually equivalent to the point forecast. Yet that distribution also has a spread, representing the remaining uncertainty around the point forecast. Good forecasting processes will communicate this spread effectively; bad forecasting processes will remain silent on this issue, projecting unrealistic confidence in a single number. Further, not making explicit the inherent forecast uncertainty can lead to decision makers using both highly uncertain and highly certain

---

[1]The simplest forecasting method is naïve forecasting, which means using the most recently observed demand to predict the future (also called demand chasing). Another simple method is using a long-run average of demand to predict the future (also called demand averaging). These methods can perform well. The terms simple or naïve are not meant to describe their accuracy but only relate to their simplicity.

forecasts in a similar way. It is not uncommon, for example, for firms to require equivalent safety stocks across different products, even though the uncertainty inherent in these products may vary vastly. The root cause of this problem often lies in insufficient reporting of uncertainty. We will further explore the idea of probabilistic forecasting in Chapters 2 and 3.

The effective design of forecasting processes seems difficult, but the benefits of getting the forecasting process right are tremendous. Fixing the forecasting process is a managerial challenge that usually does not require major financial investments. The challenge of improving the forecasting process often does not lie in the risks of investing into advanced machines or information technology or the costs of hiring more people and expanding the organization. Rather, the challenge is to manage cross-functional communication and push through change despite a multitude of stakeholders (Smith 2009). Yet, if these challenges are overcome, the returns can be huge. For example, Oliva and Watson (2009) document that the improvement of a forecasting process at an electronics manufacturing company led to a doubling of inventory turns and a decrease of 50 percent in on-hand inventory. Similarly, Clarke (2006) documents how the major overhaul of the forecasting process at Coca Cola Inc. led to a 25 percent reduction in days of inventory. These are supply chain improvements that would otherwise require significant investments into technology to achieve; if an organizational change (though challenging and time-consuming) of the forecasting process can achieve similar objectives, every manager should take the opportunity to improve forecasting processes seriously.

1.2. Software

While we often highlight the managerial aspects of forecasting in this book, we also delve into the statistics of forecasting. Our goal in doing so is to provide a basic intuition to managers as to how forecasting algorithms work—to shine some light into this black box. In this context, we emphasize that this book does not assume the use of any particular forecasting software. There is a large set to choose from when selecting a forecasting software, and a comprehensive review of the features, strengths, and weaknesses of all commercially available products is beyond the scope of this book. For an overview, interested readers may visit the OR/MS biannual survey of forecasting software (www.orms-today.org/surveys/FSS/fss-fr.html).

Throughout the book, we often provide a reference to functions in Microsoft Excel to help readers implement some ideas from the book. This spreadsheet modeling software is widely available, and most managers will have a copy installed on their laptops or tablets. However, Excel is known to suffer from inaccuracies, both in its statistical and optimization functions (Mélard 2014). Further, the standard functionality of Excel only allows for very limited time series analysis, and therefore the use of Excel for forecasting inevitably requires some coding and manual entry of formulas. It is very hard to maintain a consistent forecasting process in Excel, particularly when a company is growing. Spreadsheets start accumulating errors and undocumented changes over time (Singh 2013). When implemented correctly, spreadsheets have the advantage of being very transparent. Commercially available forecasting software, on the contrary, can often have a black-box character. As such, Excel is a good complementary tool for forecasting—to learn, to communicate, and to test out new ideas—but it should not become a standard tool for forecasting in an organization in the long run.

An important alternative is the free statistical software R (www.r-project .org/). While R is more difficult to learn and use than Excel, its functionality is much broader, and through user-written content, many existing forecasting methods are available for free in R (Kolassa and Hyndman 2010). Furthermore, interface add-ons like R-Studio (www.rstudio.com/) make the software more accessible, and excellent introductory books to R from a forecasting perspective are available (e.g., Shmueli and Lichtendahl 2015).

1.3. Key Takeaways

- Almost every business decision is about the future and is thus based on forecasts. We *need* forecasts. We cannot eliminate forecasts, but we can question whether we have an effective forecasting process that makes use of all available information within our organization and supply chain.
- Different time series will differ in terms of how hard they are to predict. Inaccurate forecasts may be a result of an ineffective

forecasting process or may simply be due to the unpredictable nature of a particular business.

- No forecast is perfect. We need to directly confront, quantify, and manage the uncertainty surrounding our forecasts. Failure to communicate this uncertainty makes risk management associated with the forecast ineffective.

- Fixing the forecasting process can lead to huge improvements in the supply chain without major investments into technology. The challenge is to manage cross-functional communications and to overcome organizational silos and conflicting incentives.

CHAPTER 2

Choice Under Uncertainty

2.1. Forecasting Methods

A forecast is an input to support decision making under uncertainty. Forecasts are created by a statistical model and/or by human judgment. A statistical model is nothing but an algorithm, often embedded into a spreadsheet model or other software, which converts data into a forecast. Of course, choosing which algorithm an organization uses for forecasting and how this algorithm is implemented often requires the use of human judgment as well. However, when we examine the role of human judgment in forecasting, we mean that judgment is used in lieu of or in combination with a statistical forecast. Human judgment is thus the intuition and cognition that decision makers can employ to convert all available data and tacit information into a forecast. Both statistical models and human judgment will be discussed in much more detail in the rest of this book. In reality, most forecasting processes contain elements of both. A statistical forecast may serve as the basis of discussion, but this forecast is then revised in some form or other through human judgment to arrive at a consensus forecast, that is, a combination of different existing forecasts (statistical or judgmental) within the organization. A recent survey of professional forecasters found that while 16 percent of forecasters relied exclusively on human judgment and 29 percent depended exclusively on statistical methods, the remaining 55 percent used either a combination of judgment and statistical forecast or a judgmentally adjusted statistical forecast (Fildes and Petropoulos 2015). Another study of a major pharmaceutical company found that more than 50 percent of the forecasting experts answering the survey did not rely on the company's statistical models when preparing their forecast (Boulaksil and Franses 2009).

Forecasting in practice is thus not an automated process but is strongly influenced by the people involved in the process.[1]

Throughout this book, we will refer to a forecasting method very generally as the process through which an organization generates a forecast. This forecast does not need to be the final consensus forecast, although the consensus forecast is generated by some method. The beauty of any forecasting method is that its accuracy can be judged ex post and compared against other methods. There is always an objective realization of demand that can and should be compared to create a picture of forecast accuracy over time. Of course, this comparison should never be based on small samples. However, if a forecasting method repeatedly creates forecasts that are far off from the actual demand realizations, this observation is evidence that the method does not work well, particularly if there also is evidence that another method works better. In other words, the question of whether a forecasting method is good or bad is not a question of belief but ultimately a question of scientific empirical comparison. If the forecastability of the underlying demand is challenging, then multiple methods will fail in improving accuracy. We will explore how to make such a forecasting comparison in more detail in Chapter 12.

One key distinction that we will emphasize throughout the book is that the forecast itself is not a target or a budget or a plan. A forecast is simply an expression or belief about the most likely state of the future.[2] Targets, budgets, or plans are decisions based on forecasts, but these concepts should not be confused with the forecast itself. For example, our point forecast for demand for a particular item we want to sell on the market may be 100K units. However, it may make sense for us to set our sales representative a target of selling 110K units to motivate them to do their best. In addition, it may also make sense to plan for ordering 120K

---

[1]There are, however, exceptions to this observation. Retail organizations can have operations with more than 20,000 stock-keeping units (SKUs) that need to be forecast on a daily basis for hundreds or thousands of stores. Naturally, forecasting at this level tends to be a more automated task.

[2]The most likely state is the mode of a distribution. Many forecasting methods actually predict the mean of a distribution, which is different from the mode if the distribution is skewed.

units from our contract manufacturer, since there is a chance that demand is higher and we want to balance the risk of stocking out against the risk of having excess inventory. To make the latter decision effectively, we would, of course, also include data on ordering and sales costs, as well as assumptions on how customers would react to stockouts and how quickly the product may or may not become obsolete.

2.2. Reporting Forecast Uncertainty

This leads to another important distinction. Most firms operate with point forecasts—single numbers that express the most likely outcome on the market. Yet, we all understand that such a notion is somewhat ridiculous; the point forecast is unlikely to be realized exactly. There can be immense uncertainty in a forecast. Reporting only a point forecast communicates an illusion of certainty. Let us recall a famous quote by Goethe: "to be uncertain is to be uncomfortable, but to be certain is to be ridiculous." Point forecasts in that sense are misleading. It is much more useful and complete to report forecasts in the form of a probability distribution or at least in the form of prediction intervals, that is, best case, worst case, and most likely scenarios.

Creating such prediction intervals requires a measure of uncertainty in the forecast. While we will explore this topic in detail in Chapter 3, we provide a brief and stylized introduction here. Uncertainty is usually expressed as a standard deviation (usually abbreviated by the Greek letter σ). Given a history of past forecast errors, measuring this uncertainty is fairly straightforward—the simplest form would be to calculate the population standard deviation (= STDEV.P function in Excel) of past observed forecast errors (see Chapter 11 for a more in-depth treatment of measuring the accuracy of forecasts). Assuming that forecast errors are roughly symmetric,[3] that is, overforecasting is as likely and extensive as underfore-

---

[3]Symmetry of forecast errors is not always the case in practice, and assumed here only to make the argument simple. For example, items with low demand are naturally censored through the origin (= 0), creating a skewed error distribution; similarly if political influence within the organization creates an incentive to over- or underforecast, the distribution of errors can be skewed. Chapter 11 will examine how to detect such forecast bias in more depth.

casting, we can then conceptualize the point forecast as the center (i.e., the mean, median, and most likely value, abbreviated by the Greek letter μ) of a probability distribution, with the standard deviation σ measuring the spread of that probability distribution.

These concepts are illustrated in Figure 2.1. Suppose our forecasting method generated a point forecast of 500. From past data, we calculate a standard deviation of our past forecast errors as 20. We can thus conceptualize our forecast as a probability distribution with a mean of 500 and a standard deviation of 20 (in this illustration, we assumed a normal distribution, drawn with the Excel function = NORM.DIST). A probability distribution is nothing but a function that maps possible outcomes to probabilities.[4] For example, one could ask the question: What is the probability that demand is between 490 and 510? The area under the distribution curve between the X values of 490 and 510 would provide the answer—or alternatively the Excel function call = NORM.DIST(510;500;20;TRUE)-NORM.DIST(490;500;20;TRUE). The probability distribution thus communicates a good sense for the possible outcomes and the uncertainty associated with a forecast.

How should we report such a probabilistic forecast? Usually we do not draw the actual distribution, since this may be too much information to digest for decision makers. Reporting a standard deviation in addition to the point forecast can be difficult to interpret as well. A good practice is to report 95 percent or 80 percent prediction intervals, that is, intervals in which we are 95 or 80 percent sure that demand will fall.[5] Assuming a normal distribution, calculating such intervals is relatively easy, since a 95

---

[4]The mathematically more apt readers will notice that the y-axis of a probability distribution measures the density, not the probability of an event. While this distinction is theoretically an important one, we will refer to density as probability here, and this simplification is hopefully excused.

[5]Prediction intervals are often confused with confidence intervals (Soyer and Hogarth 2012). While a confidence interval represents the uncertainty about an estimate of a parameter of a distribution (i.e., the mean of the above distribution), a prediction interval represents the uncertainty about a draw from that distribution (i.e., demand taking certain values in the above distribution). The confidence interval for the mean is much smaller (depending on how many observations we used to estimate the mean) than the prediction interval characterizing the distribution.

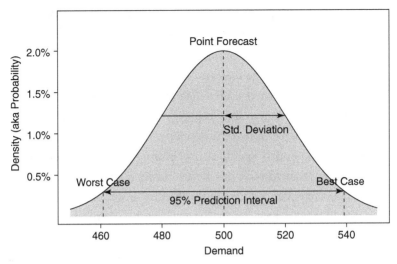

Figure 2.1 Forecasts from a probabilistic perspective

percent prediction interval means going approximately 2 standard deviations above and below the point forecast.[6] In other words, if our point forecast is 500 and the standard deviation of our forecast errors is 20, a 95 percent prediction interval is approximately [500 − 2 × 20, 500 + 2 × 20]. These end points can then be referred to as best-case and worst-case scenarios. However, one has to realize that better-than-best or worse-than-worst-case scenarios are possible, since by definition only 95 percent of the density of the probability distribution fall into the prediction interval (as also shown in Figure 2.1).

Reporting and understanding prediction intervals requires some effort. However, their calculation and reporting can be largely automated in modern forecasting software. Not reporting (or ignoring) such intervals can have distinct disadvantages for organizational decision making. Reading a point forecast without a measure of uncertainty gives you no idea how much uncertainty there really is in the forecast. Prediction intervals provide a natural instrument for forecasters to communicate the uncertainty in their forecasts adequately and for decision makers to then

---

[6]Prediction intervals like this are generally too narrow (Chatfield 2001). The reason is that these intervals often do not include the uncertainty of choosing the correct model and the uncertainty of the environment changing.

decide how to best manage the risk inherent in their decision. The consequences of not making forecast uncertainty explicit can be dramatic. At best, decision makers will form their own judgment about how much uncertainty is inherent in the forecast. Since human judgment in this context generally suffers from overconfidence (Mannes and Moore 2013), not making forecast uncertainty explicit will likely lead to an underestimation of the inherent forecast uncertainty, leading to less-than-optimal safety stocks and buffers in resulting decisions. At worst, decision makers will treat the point forecast as a deterministic number and completely ignore the inherent uncertainty in the forecast, as well as any precautions they should take in their decisions to manage their demand risk.

Adopting prediction intervals in practice is challenging; one line of criticism often brought up is that it is difficult to report more than one number and that the wide range of a 95 percent prediction interval makes the interval almost meaningless. This line of reasoning, however, misinterprets the prediction interval. The range itself does contain information about probabilities as well, since values in the center of the range are more likely than values at the end. These differences can be easily visualized. The Bank of England (BoE) has moved their GDP growth and inflation forecasts completely away from point forecasts toward probability distributions and prediction intervals. An example of how the bank reports these in a fan plot is shown in Figure 2.2. The chart contains the BoE's forecasts made at the end of the first quarter of 2014. While past data in the chart is represented by a time series, no point forecasts are reported. Instead, areas of different shading indicate different prediction intervals into which the actuals for the succeeding quarters are predicted to fall. Overall, Figure 2.2 is easy to interpret while summarizing a lot of information and represents the state of the art of communicating forecast uncertainty (Kreye et al. 2012).

Another line of attack against using prediction intervals is that, in the end, single numbers are needed for decision making. Ultimately, containers need to be loaded with a certain volume; capacity levels require hiring a certain number of people or buying a certain number of machines. What good is a forecast that shows a range when in the end one number is needed? This argument makes the mistake of confusing the forecast with decision making. The forecast is an input into a decision, but not a

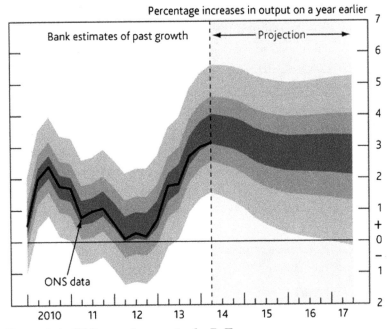

Figure 2.2 *GDP growth reporting by BoE*

Source: www.bankofengland.co.uk; ONS represents the Office of National Statistics.

decision per se. Firms can and must set service-level targets that translate probabilistic forecasts into single numbers.

2.3. Service Levels

Consider the following illustrative example. Suppose you are a baker and you need to decide how many bagels to bake in the morning for selling throughout the day. The variable cost to make bagels is 10 cents, and you sell them for $1.50. You donate all bagels that you do not sell during a day to a kitchen for the homeless. You estimate that demand for bagels for the day has a mean of 500 and a standard deviation of 80, giving you a 95 percent prediction interval of roughly (340, 660). How many bagels should you bake in the morning? Your point forecast is 500—but you probably realize that this would not be the right number. Baking 500 bagels would give you just a 50 percent chance of meeting all demand during the day.

This 50 percent chance represents an important concept in this decision context—the so-called type I service level or in-stock probability, that is, the likelihood of meeting all demands with your inventory.[7] This chance of not encountering a stockout is a key metric often used in organizational decision making. What service level should you strive for? The answer to that question requires carefully comparing the implications of running out of stock with the implications of having leftover inventory—that is, managing the inherent demand risk. The key concepts here are so-called overage and underage cost, that is, assessing what happens when too much or too little inventory is available. An overage situation in the case of our bagel baker implies that he/she has made bagels at a cost of $0.10 that he/she is giving away for free; this would lead to an actual loss of $0.10. An underage situation implies that he/she has not made enough bagels and thus lose a profit margin of $1.40 per bagel not sold. This is an opportunity cost—a loss of $1.40. Assuming no other costs of a stockout (i.e., loss of cross-sales, loss of goodwill, loss of reputation, etc.), this $1.40 represents the underage cost in this situation. Obviously, underage costs in this case (=$1.40) are much higher than overage costs (=$0.10), implying that you would probably bake more than 500 bagels in the morning.

Finding the right service level in this context is known as the "newsvendor problem" in the academic literature. Its solution is simple and elegant. One calculates the so-called critical fractile, which is given by the ratio of underage to the sum of underage and overage costs. In our case, this critical fractile is roughly equal to 93% (=1.40/[1.40+0.10]). The critical fractile is the optimal type I service level. In other words, considering the underage and overage costs, you should strive for a 93 percent service level in bagel baking. This service level in the long run balances the opportunity costs of running out of stock with the obsolescence costs of baking bagels that do not sell. So how many bagels should you bake? The only difficult part now is to convert the service-level target (93 percent) into a so-called z-score. In Excel, this involves evaluating the standard normal inverse function (= NORM.S.INV) at the service level, which

---

[7] It is important not to confuse type I and type II service levels. Type II service levels (also called fill rates) measure the likelihood of a customer getting the product, which is higher than the likelihood of meeting all demand with the available inventory.

in our case produces a z-score of 1.50. One then multiplies this z-score with the standard deviation of our demand forecast to obtain the safety stock needed (1.50 × 80 =120). Adding this safety stock (120) to the point forecast (500) gives the necessary inventory quantity to obtain a 93 percent service level. In other words, you should bake 620 bagels to have a 93 percent chance of meeting all demands in a day.

This example illustrates the difference between a forecast, which serves as an input into a decision, and the actual decision, which is the number of bagels to bake. The point forecast is not the decision, and making a good decision would be impossible without understanding the uncertainty inherent in the point forecast. Good decision making under uncertainty requires actively understanding uncertainty and balancing risks; in the case of our bagel baker, the key managerial task was not to influence the forecast but rather to understand the cost factors involved with different risks in the decision and then define a service level that balances these risk factors. A proper forecast made in the form of a probability distribution or a prediction interval should make this task easier. The actual quantity of bagels baked is simply a function of the forecast and the service level.

Our previous discussion highlights the importance of setting adequate service levels for the items in question. Decision makers should understand how their organization derives these service levels. Since the optimal service level depends on the profit margin of the product, items with different profit margins require different service levels. While overage costs are comparatively easy to measure (cost of warehousing, depreciation, insurance, etc.; see Timme 2003), underage costs involve understanding customer behavior and are thus more challenging to quantify. What happens when a customer desires a product that is unavailable? In the best case, the customer finds and buys a substitute product, which may have been sold at a higher margin, or puts the item on backorder. In the worst case, the customer takes their business elsewhere and tweets about the bad service experience. Studies of mail order catalog businesses show that the indirect costs of a stockout—that is, the opportunity costs from lost cross-sales and reduced long-term sales of the customer—are almost twice as high as the lost revenue from the stockout itself (Anderson, Fitzsimons, and Simester 2006). Similar consequences of stockouts threaten profitability in supermarkets (Corsten and Gruen 2004). The task of setting service levels thus requires studying customer behavior and understanding the revenue risks associated with a stockout. Since this challenge can appear daunting, managers can sometimes react in a knee-jerk fashion and simply set very high service levels (=99.99%). Such an approach in turn leads to excessive inventory levels and corresponding inventory holding costs. Achieving the right balance between customer service and inventory holding ultimately requires a careful analysis and thorough understanding of the business.

Note that while we use inventory management as an example of decision making under uncertainty here, a similar rationale of differentiating between forecast and related decision making applies in other decision-making contexts as well. For example, in service staffing decisions, the forecast relates to customer demand in a certain time period and the decision is how much service capacity to put in place—too much capacity means money wasted in salaries, and too little capacity means wait times and possibly lost sales due to customers avoiding the service system due to inconvenient queues or inadequate service. Similarly, in project management, a forecast may involve predicting how long the project will take and finding how much time buffer is available to build into the schedule. Too large a buffer may result in wasted resources and lost revenue, whereas too little buffer may lead to projects exceeding their deadlines and resulting contractual fines. One has to understand that forecasting itself is not risk management—forecasting simply supports the decision that managers take by carefully balancing the risk inherent in their choice under uncertainty.

Actual inventory management systems are more complex than the examples in this chapter may suggest, since they require adjusting for fixed costs of ordering (i.e., shipping and container filling), uncertain supply lead times (e.g., by ordering from overseas), best by dates and obsolescence, optimization possibilities (like rebates or discounts on large orders), contractually agreed order quantities, as well as dependent demand items (i.e., scheduling production for one unit requires ordering the whole bill of materials). A thorough review of inventory management techniques is beyond the scope of this book, and interested readers are referred to Nahmias and Olsen (2015) for a thorough overview.

2.4. Key Takeaways

- Forecasts are not targets or budgets or plans; these are different concepts that need to be kept apart within organizations, or confusion will occur.

- Often the word "forecast" is shorthand for "point forecast." However, point forecasts are almost never perfectly accurate. We need to measure and communicate the uncertainty associated with our forecast. To accomplish this, we calculate prediction intervals, which we can visualize using fan plots.

- A key concept required to convert a forecast into a decision is the service level, that is, the likelihood of meeting an uncertain demand with a fixed quantity. These service levels represent key managerial decisions and should balance the risk of not having enough units available (underage) with the risk of having too many units available (overage).

CHAPTER 3

A Simple Example

To bring forecasting to life, our objective in this chapter is to provide readers with a short and simple example of how to apply and interpret a statistical forecasting method in practice. This example is stylized and illustrative only—in reality, forecasting is messier, but it serves as a guideline of how to think about and successfully execute a forecasting method and apply it for decision making.

3.1. Point Forecasts

Suppose you are interested in predicting weekly demand for a particular product. Specifically, you have historical data from the past 50 weeks and you want to get a forecast for how demand for your product will develop over the next 10 weeks, that is, weeks 51 to 60 (see Figure 3.1). Completing this task means making 10 different forecasts; the one-step-ahead forecast is your forecast for week 51; the two-step-ahead forecast is your forecast for week 52; and so forth. You can assume that there is no trend and no seasonality in the data, just to keep things simple. Trends and seasonality are predictable patterns in the data, and we will examine them in more detail in Chapter 5.[1] Further, you have no additional information on the market available beyond this history of demand (Chapter 8 will examine how to use additional information to achieve better predictions). A time series plot of your data is shown in Figure 3.1.

---

[1]Note that the time series in Figure 3.1 appears as if it contains a positive trend, since the points on the right-hand side of the graph are higher than the points on the left-hand side. This is sometimes referred to as illusionary trend perception (Kremer, Moritz, and Siemsen 2011). The data series here was artificially created using a random walk with noise, and the shifts in demand inherent in such a random walk can make us believe in an illusionary trend in the data.

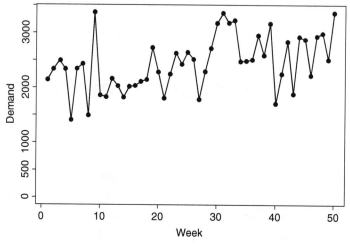

Figure 3.1 Time series for our example

Two simple approaches to forecasting would be to create a point fore-cast by either taking the most recent observation of demand (= 3370) or calculating the long-run average over all available data points (= 2444). Both approaches tend to ignore the distinct shape of the data of the series; note that the time series starts at a somewhat low level and then exhibits an upward shift. Calculating the long-run average ignores the observation that the time series currently seems to hover at a higher level than in the past. Conversely, taking only the most recent demand observation as your forecast ignores the fact that the last observation is very close to an all-time high and that historically an all-time high has usually not signaled a persistent upward shift, but has been followed by lower demands in the weeks immediately following—a simple case of regression to the mean. You could, of course, simply split the data and calculate the average de-mand over the last 15 periods (= 2652). Not a bad approach—but the choice of how far back to go (= 15 periods) seems ad hoc. Why should the last 15 observations receive equal weights and those before receive no weight at all? Further, this approach does not fully capture the possibil-ity that you could encounter a shift in the data; going further back into the past allows your forecast—particularly your prediction intervals—to reflect the uncertainty of further shifts in the level of the series occurring.

A weighted average over all available demand data would solve these issues, with more recent data receiving more weight than older data.

What would be good weights, and if I have 50 time periods of past data, do I really need to specify 50 different weights? It turns out that there is a simple method to create such weighted averages, which also turns out to be the method to use for this kind of time series: single exponential smoothing. Chapter 6 will provide more details on this method; for now, understand that a key aspect of this method is that it uses a so-called smoothing parameter α (alpha). The higher α, the higher the weight given to recent as opposed to earlier data when calculating a forecast. The lower α, the more the forecast takes the whole demand history into account without heavily discounting older data. In this case, if you feed the 50 time periods into an exponential smoothing model to estimate an optimal smoothing parameter, you will obtain an α value of 0.16—indicating that there is some degree of instability and change in the data (which we clearly see in Figure 3.1), but also some noise; one-step-ahead forecasts under exponential smoothing become a weighted average between most recently observed demand (weight = 0.16) and the most recent forecast made by the method (weight $= 1 - 0.16 = 0.84$).

Now you are probably thinking: Wait! I have to create a weighted average between two numbers, where one of these numbers is my most recent forecast. But I have not made any forecasts yet! If the method assumes a current forecast and I have not made forecasts in the past using this method, what do I do? The answer is simple. You use the most recent fitted forecasts. In other words, suppose you had started in week 2 with a naïve forecast of your most recent demand and applied the exponential smoothing method ever since to create forecasts, what would have been your most recent forecast for week 50? Figure 3.2 provides an overview of how these fitted forecasts would have looked like.

Note that these fitted forecasts are not real forecasts; you used the data of the last 50 weeks to estimate a smoothing parameter. You then used this parameter in turn to generate fitted forecasts for the last 50 periods. You would not have known this smoothing parameter in week 1, since you did not have enough data available to estimate it. Thus, the recorded fitted forecast for week 2, supposedly calculated in week 1, would not have been possible to make in week 1. Nevertheless, this method of generating fitted forecasts now allows you to make a forecast for week 51. Specifically, you take your most recent demand observation (= 3370) and your most recent "fitted"

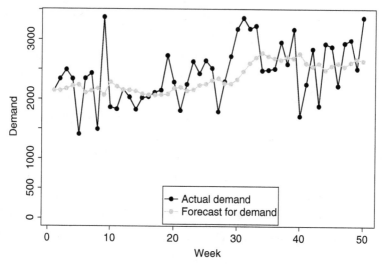

Figure 3.2 Demand forecasts for our example

forecast (=2643) and calculate the weighted average of these two numbers
(0.16 × 3370 + 0.84 × 2643 = 2759) as your point forecast for week 51.

So, what about the remaining nine point forecasts for periods 52 to 60?
The answer is surprisingly simple. The single exponential smoothing model
is a "level only" model, which assumes that there is no trend or seasonality
(which, as mentioned initially, is correct for this time series, since it was
constructed with neither trend nor seasonality). Without such additional
time series components (see Chapter 5), the point forecast for the time series remains flat, that is, the same number. Moving further out in the time
horizon may influence the spread of our forecast probability distribution,
but in this case, the center of that distribution—and therefore the point
forecast—remains the same. Our forecasts for the next 10 weeks are thus
a flat line of 2759 for weeks 51 to 60. Your two-step-ahead, three-step-
ahead, and later point forecasts are equal to your one-step-ahead point
forecast. Your intuition may tell you that this is odd; indeed, intuitively,
many believe that the form of the time series of forecasts should be similar
to the form of the time series of demand (Harvey 1995). Yet this is one
of those instances where our intuition fails us; the time series contains
noise, which is the unpredictable component of demand. A good forecast
filters out this noise (an aspect that is clearly visible in Figure 3.2). Thus,
the time series of forecasts becomes less variable than the actual time series

of demand. In our case, there simply is no information available to tell us whether the time series will shift up, shift down, or stay at the same level. In the absence of such information, our most likely prediction of demand falls into the center—that is, to a prediction that the time series stays at the same level. Thus, the point forecast remains constant as we predict further into the future. Only the uncertainty associated with this forecast may change as our predictions reach further out into the unknown.

3.2. Prediction Intervals

So how to calculate a prediction interval associated with our point forecasts? We will use this opportunity to explore three different methods of calculating prediction intervals: (1) using the standard deviation of observed forecast errors, (2) using the empirical distribution of forecast errors, and (3) using theory-based formulas.

The first method is the simplest and most intuitive one. It is easy to calculate the errors associated with our past "fitted" forecasts by calculating the difference between actual demand and fitted forecasts in each period. Note that if we take the average of the absolute values (also called mean absolute error, or MAE) or of the squared values (also called mean squared error, or MSE) of these forecast errors, we can calculate standard measures of forecast accuracy (see Chapter 11). For our purposes, we can calculate the population standard deviation of these forecast errors (σ = 464.63).[2] This value represents the spread of possible outcomes around our point forecast (see Figure 2.1). If we want to, for example, calculate an 80 percent prediction interval around the point forecast, we have to figure out the z-score associated with the lowest 10 percent of the probability distribution—10 percent, because an 80 percent interval around the point forecast excludes the lower and upper 10 percent of the distribution. The corresponding z-score is –1.28/+1.28, and we thus subtract 1.28 and add 1.28 times our standard deviation estimate (= 464.63) from or to the point forecast (= 2752) to obtain an 80 percent prediction interval of (2164;

---

[2]There is a relationship between MSE and σ. If the forecasting method is unbiased, that is, the average forecast error is 0, then σ is equivalent to the square root of MSE (also called the root mean square error, or RMSE). If there is a bias in the forecasting method, then σ^2 + bias^2 is equivalent to the MSE.

3354). In other words, we can be 80 percent sure that demand in week 51 lies in between 2164 and 3354, with the most likely outcome being 2759.

Method (1) assumes that our forecast errors roughly follow a normal distribution; method (2) does not make this assumption, but generally requires more data to be effective. Consider that an 80 percent prediction interval ignores the top and the bottom 10 percent of errors that could be made. Since we have approximately 50 "fitted" forecast errors, ignoring the top and the bottom 10 percent of our errors roughly equates to ignoring the top and the bottom five (=10% × 50) errors in our data. In our data, the errors that fall just within these boundaries are (−434; 581), so another simple way of creating an 80 percent prediction interval is to simply add and subtract these two extreme errors from and to the point forecast to generate a prediction interval of (2325; 3340), which is a bit more narrow than our previously calculated interval from method (1). In practice, bootstrapping techniques exist that increase the effectiveness of this method in terms of creating prediction intervals.

The final method (3) only exists for forecasting methods that have an underlying theoretical model.[3] A key to estimate uncertainty in this method is that if a theoretical model underlies the method, one can theoretically calculate the standard deviation of the forecast error; in the case of single exponential smoothing, this formula has a comparatively simple form: If one predicts h time periods into the future, the underlying standard deviation of the forecast error can be calculated by taking the one-period-ahead forecast error standard deviation as calculated in method (1) and multiplying it by $1+(h-1) \times \alpha^2$. This is a relatively simple formula; similar formulas exist for other methods but can be more complex.

This leads to an interesting discussion. How does one calculate the standard deviation of forecasts that are not one-step-ahead but h steps ahead? If we prepare a forecast in week 50 for week 52 and if we use the standard deviation of forecast errors for one-step-ahead forecasts resulting from method

---

[3]Note that any way of coming up with a forecast is a forecasting method; a forecasting model exists only if this forecasting method is derived from a theoretical model that specifies the statistical process generating the data. Such model-based forecasting methods include the exponential smoothing methods discussed in Chapter 6 and the ARIMA methods discussed in Chapter 7. Croston's method, which is described in Chapter 9, is an example of a forecasting method without a model.

(1), our estimated forecast uncertainty will generally underestimate the true uncertainty in this two-step-ahead forecast. Unless a time series is entirely stable and has no changing components, predicting further into the future implies an increasing likelihood that the time series will move to a different level as we forecast further out in time. The formula mentioned in method (3) would therefore see the standard deviation of the one-step-ahead forecast error for period 51 (= 464.63) increase to 476.52 for the two-step-ahead forecast error for week 52 and to 488.42 for the three-step-ahead forecast error for week 53. Prediction intervals increase accordingly.

Another approach would be to calculate the two-step-ahead fitted forecasts for all past demands. In the case of single exponential smoothing, the one-step-ahead forecast is equal to the two-step-ahead forecast, but error calculation now requires comparing this forecast to demand one period later. The resulting error standard deviations for the two-step-ahead forecast (= 478.04) and three-step-ahead forecast (= 489.34) are slightly higher than those for the one-step-ahead forecast and the adjusted standard deviations using the formula from method (3).

Forecasting software will usually provide one or more of these methods to calculate prediction intervals and will allow visualizing them. For instance, Figure 3.3 shows point forecasts and 70 percent prediction intervals from method (3).

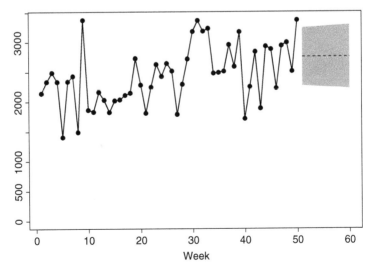

Figure 3.3 Demand, point forecasts, and prediction intervals

So what is the right method to use? How do we come up with the right prediction interval? Which standard deviation estimate works best? The common criticism against method (1) is that it underestimates the uncertainty about the true forecasting model and does not incorporate the notion that the model could change. Standard errors are thus too low. Method (2) requires a lot of data to be effective. Method (3) is usually based on some assumptions and may not be robust if these assumptions are not met. In practice, getting the right method to calculate prediction intervals can require careful calibration and selection from different methods. Chapter 11 outlines how the accuracy of prediction intervals can be assessed and, therefore, how different methods can be compared in practice. In general, though, using any of the methods described is better than using no method at all; while getting good estimates of the underlying uncertainty of a forecast can be a challenging task, any such estimate is better than assuming that there is no uncertainty in the forecast, or supposing that all forecasts have the same inherent uncertainty.

3.3. Decision Making

Given that we now understand how to estimate the parameters of a probability distribution of future demand, how would we proceed with decision making? Suppose our objective is to place an order right now, which has a lead time of 2 weeks; suppose also that we place an order every week, so that the order we place right now has to cover the demand we face in week 53; further, suppose we have perishable inventory, so that we do not need to worry about existing inventories left over from week 52 and that the inventory we have available to meet the demand in week 53 is equal to what we order right now. In this case, we would take the three-week-ahead forecast (= 2759) together with the three-week-ahead standard deviation (= 488.42) to provide a demand forecast. It is important to match the right forecast (three-week-ahead) with the right forecast uncertainty measure (three-week-ahead, and not one-week-ahead, in this case). Suppose we want to satisfy an 85 percent service level; the z-score associated with an 85 percent service level is 1.04. Thus, we would place an order for

$2759 + 1.04 \times 488.42 \approx 3267$ units; this order quantity would, according to our forecast, have an 85 percent chance of meeting all demand.

This concludes our simple example; key learning points for readers are to understand the mechanics of creating point forecasts and prediction intervals for time periods in the future and how these predictions can translate into decisions. We will now proceed to provide more detailed explanations of different forecasting methods.

PART II
Forecasting Basics

CHAPTER 4

Know Your Time Series

4.1. Data Availability

A time series is a sequence of similar measurements taken at regular time intervals. Time series analysis, our topic in Chapters 4, 5, 6, 7, and 9, means examining the history of the time series itself to gather information about the future. An inherent assumption in time series analysis is that the past of a series contains information about the future of the same series. Regression modeling, which is our topic in Chapter 8, means using the information contained in another data series to make predictions about the future of a focal time series.

One essential aspect of time series forecasting is that time needs to be "bucketed" into time periods. Many demand forecasts are made on a monthly basis ("how much product will our customers demand next month?"), and thus the time series requires aggregating data into monthly buckets. Note that "a month" is not an entirely regular time interval, since some months have more days than others, but for most applications, this nonregularity is inconsequential enough to be ignored. Financial forecasting works on a quarterly or yearly basis, whereas some operational forecasting requires weekly, daily, and sometimes even quarter-hourly time buckets, for example, in the case of call center traffic forecasting (Minnucci 2006). This temporal dimension of aggregation does, as we shall explain later in this chapter, imply different degrees of statistical aggregation as well, making forecasting more or less challenging. It also raises the question of temporal hierarchies (see Chapter 14), that is, at what level should the organization forecast, and how does the organization aggregate or disaggregate to longer or shorter segments of time?

Another important aspect to understand about your forecast is the availability of relevant historical data. Most methods discussed in the next chapters assume that some demand history for a time series exists. For example, if exponential smoothing is used (see Chapter 6) and the model includes seasonality, then at least nine past quarters are needed for quarterly time series models, and 17 past months are needed for monthly time series models (Hyndman and Kostenko 2007)—and these are *minimum* requirements; if the time series is very noisy, much more data is needed to get reliable estimates for the method's parameters and thus obtain dependable forecasts.[1] This data requirement may be excessive in many business contexts where the lifecycle of products is only 3 years. If lifecycles are short, changes to the product portfolio need to be carefully assessed as to whether they represent true new product introductions, that is, the introduction of a novel good or service that is incomparable to any existing product in the firm's portfolio, or a semi-new product introduction, that is, a modified version of a product the firm has sold before (Tonetti 2006). In the former case, the methods we will discuss here do not hold; forecasts will require modeling the product lifecycle, which requires good market research and extensive conjoint analysis to have a chance of being successful. Interested readers are referred to a different book by the same publisher for further information on new product forecasting (Berry 2010). In the latter case, forecasting can proceed as we discuss here, as long as some existing data can be deemed representative of the semi-new product. For example, if the semi-new product is a simple engineering change of a previous version of the product, the history of the previous version of the product should apply and can be used to initialize the forecasting method for the semi-new product. If the change is a change in packaging or style, the level of the time series may change, but other components of the series, such as the trend, seasonality, and possibly even the uncertainty in demand, may remain constant. Thus, the estimates of these components from the past can be used for the new model as initial estimates, greatly reducing the need for a data history to be available. Similarly, if the semi-new product is simply a new variant within a category, then the trend and seasonality that exists at the category level may apply to the new variant as well; in other words, smart top-down forecasting in a hierarchy

---

[1]If too little data is available, the risk of detecting seasonality where none exists is much higher than the risk of failing to detect seasonality if it exists. Shrinkage methods to better deal with seasonality in such settings are available (Miller and Williams 2003).

(see Chapter 14) can allow forecasters to learn about these time series components by looking at the collection of other, similar variants within the same category.

A first step in time series analysis is to understand what data underlies the series. Demand forecasting means making statements about future demand; the data that is stored in company databases often only shows actual sales. The difference between demand and sales comes into play during stock-outs. If inventory runs out, customers may still demand a product, so sales may be lower than the actual demand. In such a case, customers may turn to a competitor, delay their purchase, or buy a substitute product. In the latter case, the substitute's sales are actually higher than the raw demand for it. If sales are used as an input for demand forecasting, both point forecasts and their associated prediction intervals will be wrong. Modern forecasting software can adjust sales data accordingly if stock-out information is recorded. The mathematics of such adjustments are beyond the scope of this book. Interested readers are referred to Nahmias (1994) for further details.

Adjusting sales to estimate demand requires clearly understanding whether data represents sales or demand. Demand can be very difficult to observe in business-to-consumer contexts. If a product is not on the shelf, it is hard to tell whether a customer walking through the store demanded the product or not. In online retail contexts, demand can be clearly observed if inventory availability is not shown to the customers before they place an item into their shopping basket. However, if this information is presented to customers before they click on purchase, demand is again difficult to observe. Demand is generally easier to observe in business-to-business settings, since customer requests are usually recorded. In modern ERP software, salespeople usually work with an "available-to-promise" number. Running out of "available-to-promise" means that some customer requests are not converted into orders; if these requests are not recorded by the salespeople, databases again only show sales and not demand.

4.2. Stationarity

One key attribute of a time series is referred to as stationarity. Stationarity means that the mean of demand is constant over time, that the variance of demand remains constant, and that the correlation between current and most recent demand observations (and other parameters of the demand distribution) remains constant. Stationarity in essence requires that the time series has constant properties when looked at over time. Many time series violate these criteria; for example, a time series with a trend (see Chapter 5) is not stationary, since the mean demand is persistently increasing or decreasing. Similarly, a simple random walk (see Chapter 5) is not stationary since mean demand randomly increases or decreases in every time period. In essence, nonstationary series imply that demand conditions for a product change over time, whereas stationary series imply that demand conditions are very stable. Some forecasting methods, such as the ARIMA methods discussed in Chapter 7, work well only if the underlying time series is stationary.

Time series are often transformed to become stationary before they are analyzed. Typical data transformations include first differencing, that is, examining only the changes of demand between consecutive time periods; calculating growth rates, that is, examining the normalized first difference; or taking the natural logarithm of the data. Suppose, for example, one observes the following four observations of a time series: 100, 120, 160, and 150. The corresponding three observations of the first difference series become 20, 40, and -10. Expressed as growth rates, this series of first differences becomes 20, 33, and -6 percent.

Essential to these transformations is that they are reversible. While estimations are made on the transformed data, the resulting forecasts can be easily transformed back to apply to the untransformed time series. The benefit of such transformations usually lies in the reduction of variability and in filtering out the unstable portions of the data. There are several statistical tests for stationarity that will usually be reported in statistical software, such as the Dickey–Fuller test. It is useful to apply these tests to examine whether a first-differenced time series has achieved stationarity or not.

A common mistake in managerial thinking is to assume that using "old" data (i.e., 4–5 years ago) for forecasting is bad, since obviously so much has changed since then. Modern forecasting techniques will deal with this change without excluding the data; in fact, they need data that shows how much has changed over time, otherwise the methods may underestimate how much the future can change from the present. Excluding data is rarely a good practice in forecasting. A long history of data allows the forecaster and his/her methods to more clearly assess market volatility and change.

4.3. Forecastability and Scale

Another aspect to understand about a time series is the forecastability of the series. As discussed in Chapter 1, some time series contain more noise than others, making the task of predicting their future realizations more challenging. The less forecastable a time series is, the wider the prediction interval associated with the forecast will be. Understanding the forecastability of a series not only helps in terms of setting expectations among decision makers, but is also important when examining appropriate benchmarks for forecasting performance. A competitor may be more accurate at forecasting if they have a better forecasting process or if their time series are more forecastable. The latter may simply be a fact of them operating at a larger scale, with less variety, or their products being less influenced by current fashion and changing consumer trends.

One metric that is used to measure the forecastability of a time series is to calculate the ratio of the standard deviation of the time series data itself to the standard deviation of forecast errors using a benchmark method (Hill, Zhang, and Burch 2015). The logic behind this ratio is that the standard deviation of demand is in some sense a lower bound on forecasting performance since it generally corresponds to using a simple, long-run average as your forecasting method for the future. Any useful forecasting method should not lead to more uncertainty than the uncertainty inherent in demand. Thus, if this ratio is >1, forecasting in a time series can benefit from more complex methods than using a long-run average. If this ratio is close to 1 (or even <1), the time series currently cannot be forecast any better than using a long-run average.

This conceptualization is very similar to what some researchers call "Forecast Value Added" (Gilliland 2013). In this concept, one defines a base accuracy for a time series by calculating the forecast accuracy achieved (see Chapter 11) by the best simple method—either using a long-run average or the most recent demand—to predict the future.

Every step in the forecasting process, whether it is the output of a statistical forecasting model, the consensus forecast from a group, or the judgmental adjustment to a forecast by a higher level executive, is then benchmarked in terms of their long-run error against this base accuracy; if a method requires effort from the organization but does not lead to better forecast accuracy compared to a method that requires less effort, it can be eliminated from future forecasting processes. Results from such comparisons are often sobering—some estimates suggest that in almost 50 percent of time series, the existing toolset available for forecasting does not improve upon simple forecasting methods (Morlidge 2014). In other words, demand averaging or simple demand chasing may sometimes be the best a forecaster can do to create predictions.

Some studies examine what drives the forecastability of a time series (Schubert 2012). Key factors here include the overall volume of sales (larger volume means more aggregation of demand, thus less observed noise), the coefficient of variation of the series (more variability relative to mean demand), and the intermittency of data (data with only few customers that place large orders is more difficult to predict than data with many customers that place small orders). In a nutshell, the forecastability of a time series can be explained by characteristics of the product as well as characteristics of the firm within its industry. There are economies of scale in forecasting, with forecasting at higher volumes being generally easier than forecasting for very low volumes.

The source of these economies of scale lies in the principle of statistical aggregation. Imagine trying to forecast who among all the people living in your street will buy a sweater this week. You would end up with a forecast for each person living in the street that is highly uncertain for each individual. However, if you just want to forecast how many people living in your street buy a sweater in total, the task becomes much easier. At the individual level, you can make many errors, but at the aggregate level, these errors cancel out. This effect will increase the more you aggregate—that is, predicting at the neighborhood, city, county, state, region, or country level. Thus, the forecastability of a series is often a question of the level of aggregation that a time series is focused on. Very disaggregate series can become intermittent and thus very challenging to forecast (see Chapter 9 for details). Very aggregate series are easier to forecast, but if the level of aggregation is too high, these forecasts become less useful for planning purposes as the information they contain is not detailed enough.

It is important in this context to highlight the difference between relative and absolute comparisons in forecast accuracy. In absolute terms, a higher level of aggregation will have more uncertainty than each individual series, but in relative terms, the uncertainty at the aggregate level will be less than the sum of the uncertainties at the lower level. If you predict whether a person buys a sweater or not, your absolute error is at most 1, whereas the maximum error of predicting how many people in your street buy a sweater or not depends on how many people live in your street; nevertheless, the sum of the errors you make at the individual level will be less than the error you make in the sum. For example, suppose five people live in your street, and we can order them by how far into the street (i.e. first house, second house, etc.) they live. You predict that the first two residents buy a sweater, whereas the last three do not. Your aggregate prediction is just that two residents buy a sweater. Suppose now, actually only the last two residents buy a sweater. Your forecast is 100 percent accurate at the aggregate level, but only 20 percent accurate at the disaggregate level. In general, the standard deviation of forecast errors at the aggregate level will be less than the sum of the standard deviations of forecast errors made at the disaggregate level.

The ability to use more aggregate forecasts in planning can also be achieved through product and supply chain design, and the benefits of aggregation here are not limited to better forecasting performance but also include reduced inventory costs. For example, the concept of postponement in supply chain design favors postponing the differentiation of products until later in the process. This enables forecasting and planning at higher levels of aggregation for longer within the supply chain. Paint companies were early adopters of this idea by producing generic colors that are then mixed into the final product at the retail level. This allows forecasting (and stocking) at much higher levels of aggregation. Similarly, Hewlett-Packard demonstrated how to use distribution centers for the localization of their products in order to produce and ship generic printers into the distribution centers. A product design strategy that aims for better aggregation is component commonality, or so-called platform strategies. Here, components across SKUs are kept in common, enabling production and procurement to operate with forecasts and plans at a higher level of aggregation. Volkswagen is famous for pushing the boundaries of this approach with its MQB platform, which allows component sharing and final assembly on the same line across such diverse cars as the Audi A3 and the Volkswagen Touran. Additive manufacturing may become a technology that allows planning at very aggregate levels (e.g., printing raw materials and flexible printing capacity), thereby allowing companies to deliver a variety of products without losing economies of scale in forecasting and inventory planning.

4.4. Key Takeaways

- Understanding your data is the first step to a good forecast.
- The objective of most forecasts is to predict demand, yet the data available to prepare these forecasts often reflects sales; if stock-outs occur, sales are less than demand.
- Many forecasting methods require time series to be stationary, that is, to have constant parameters over time. Stationarity can often be achieved by suitable transformations of the original time series such as differencing the series.
- A key attribute of a time series is its forecastability. Your competitors may have more accurate forecasts because their forecasting process is better or because their time series are more forecastable.
- There are economies of scale in forecasting; predicting at a larger scale tends to be easier due to statistical aggregation effects.

CHAPTER 5

Time Series Decomposition

5.1. Components of a Series

Decomposition is a management technique for complexity reduction. Separating a problem into its components and then solving the components separately before reassembling the components into a larger decision enables better decision making (e.g., Raiffa 1968). The key idea in our forecasting application is to "decompose" a time series into separate components that can be examined and estimated separately. These components can then be recombined to generate a forecast. Many forecasting methods either require data that has already been decomposed or incorporate a decomposition approach directly into the method.

The components usually examined in a time series analysis are the *level*, the *trend*, the *seasonality*, and *random noise*. Historically, the business cycle was sometimes seen as an additional component in time series, but since estimating the business cycle and predicting when the cycle turns is inherently very challenging, many time series models do not explicitly consider the business cycle as a separate time series component anymore.

The level of a time series describes the center of the series at any point. That is, if we could imagine a time series where random noise, trend, and seasonality are taken out of the equation, the remainder of the series would be the level.

A trend describes predictable increases or decreases in the level of a series. A time series that grows or declines in a large number of successive time periods has a trend. By definition, trends need to be somewhat stable to allow predictability; it is often a challenge to differentiate a trend from abrupt shifts in the level, as we have discussed in Chapter 3. One can only speak of a trend, as opposed to an abrupt level shift, if one has a reasonable expectation that the shift in the level reoccurs again in a similar fashion in the next time period. A long-run persistence of such increases/ decreases in the data is necessary to establish that a real trend exists.

A trend in the time series can have many underlying causes. A product at the beginning of its lifecycle will experience a positive trend as more and more customers receive information about the product and decide to buy it. On the upside of the business cycle, gross domestic product expands, making consumers wealthier and more able to purchase. More fundamentally, the world population is currently growing every year. A firm that sells products globally should to some degree observe this increase in the world population as a trend in their demand patterns.

Seasonality refers to a pattern of predictable and recurring shifts in the level of a time series. Examples include predictable increases in demand for consumer products every December for the holiday season, or increases in demand for air-conditioning units or ice cream during the summer. A company's regular promotion event in May will also appear as seasonality. The causes of seasonality often depend on the time frame being studied. Yearly data usually has little seasonality. While leap years create a regularity that reappears every 4 years by including an extra day, this effect is often small enough to be ignored. Monthly or quarterly data is often influenced by "time of year" or temperature effects. Weekly or daily data can additionally be subject to payday, billing cycle, and "end of month" effects (Rickwalder 2006). Hourly data will often have visible "lunchtime" effects. All these effects are treated as seasonality in time series forecasting, since they represent predictable recurring patterns over time.

5.2. Decomposition Methods

When interpreting publicly available time series, such as data from the Bureau of Labor Statistics (www.bls.gov), one needs to carefully understand whether or not seasonality has been taken out of the data already. Most government data is reported as "seasonally adjusted," implying that the seasonal component has been removed from the series. This decomposition is usually applied to the time series to avoid readers overinterpreting month-to-month changes that are driven by seasonality.

Methods to remove seasonality and trends from a time series are available in most commercial software. Taking seasonality and trends out of a time series is also easy to accomplish in spreadsheet modeling software such as Excel. Take monthly data as an example. As a first step, calculate the average demand over all data points and then calculate the average demand for each month (i.e., average demand in January, February, etc.). Dividing average monthly demand by the overall average demand creates a seasonal index. Then dividing all demand observations in the time series by the corresponding seasonal index creates a deseasonalized series. The results of such a seasonal adjustment process are illustrated in Figure 5.1.

In a similar fashion, the data can be detrended by first calculating the average first difference between observations of the series and then subtracting (n-1) times this average from the nth observation in the time series. For example, take the following time series: 100, 120, 140, and 160. The first differences of the series are 20, 20, and 20, with an average of 20. The detrended series is thus $100 - 0 \times 20 = 100$, $120 - 1 \times 20 = 100$, $140 - 2 \times 20 - 100$, and $160 - 3 \times 20 = 100$.

While these methods of deseasonalizing and detrending data are simple to use and understand, they suffer from several drawbacks. For

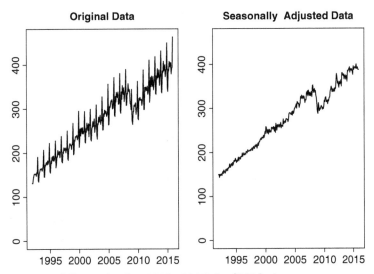

Figure 5.1 US retail sales 1992–2015 (in $US bn)

instance, they do not allow seasonality indices and trends to change over time, which makes their application challenging for longer time series. One can see in Figure 5.1, for example, that while initially our method of deseasonalizing the data removed seasonality from the series, the later part of the series show a seasonal pattern again, since the seasonal indices have changed. In shorter time series, simple methods can also be strongly influenced by outlier data. For these reasons, more sophisticated (and complex) methods have been developed. The Bureau of Labor Statistics has developed an algorithm for this purpose called X-13ARIMA-SEATS (www.census.gov/srd/www/x13as/). Software implementing this algorithm is available to download for free from the Bureau's website.

5.3. Stability of Components

The observation that seasonal components can change leads to an important discussion. The real challenge of time series analysis lies in understanding the stability of the components of a series. A perfectly stable time series is a series where the components do not change as time progresses—the level only increases through the trend, the trend remains constant, and the seasonality remains the same from year to year. If that is the case, the best time series forecasting method works with long-run averages of components. Yet time series often are inherently unstable and components change over time. The level of a series can abruptly shift as new competitors enter the market. The trend of a series can evolve over time as the product moves through its lifecycle. Even the seasonality of a series can change if underlying consumption or promotion patterns shift throughout the year.

To illustrate what change means for a time series and the implications that change has for time series forecasting, consider the two illustrative and artificially constructed time series in Figure 5.2. Both are time series without trends and seasonality (or that have been deseasonalized and detrended already). Series 1 is a series that is perfectly stable, such that month-to-month variation resembles only random noise. This is an example of data that comes from a "stationary" demand distribution and is typical for mature products. Series 2 is a time

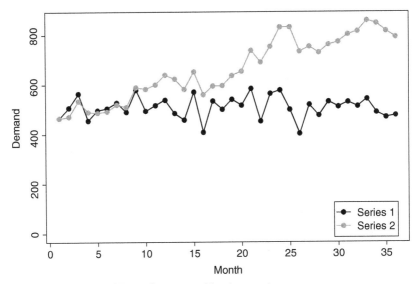

Figure 5.2 A stable and an unstable time series

series that is highly unstable, such that month-to-month variation resembles only change in the underlying level. This is an example of data that stems from a so-called random walk and is typical for prices in an efficient market. The same random draws were used to construct both series; in series 1, randomness represents just random noise around a stable level (which is at around 500 units). The best forecast for this series would be a long-run average (i.e., 500). In series 2, randomness represents random changes in the unstable level, which by the nature of randomness can push the level of the time series up or down. The best forecast in this series would be the most recent demand observation. In other words, stable time series can make use of all available data to create an estimate of the time series component and thereby create a forecast. In unstable time series, only very recent data is used for estimation, and data that is further in the past is essentially not used at all in the generation of forecasts. Differentiating between stable and unstable components, and thus using or discounting past data, is the key principle underlying exponential smoothing, which is a technique we have examined already in Chapter 3, and which we will explore further in Chapter 6.

5.4. Additive and Multiplicative Components

Another key difference to consider in a time series is how the components of the series relate to each other. The question here is whether level, trend, and seasonality are *additive* or *multiplicative*. An additive trend implies a linear increase/decrease over time, that is, an increase/decrease in demand by X units in every period. A multiplicative trend implies an exponential increase/decrease over time, that is, an increase/decrease in demand by X percent in every period. Multiplicative trends tend to be easier to interpret, since they correspond to statements like "our business grows by 10 percent every year"; however, if the trend does not change, such a statement implies exponential growth over time. Such growth patterns are common for early stages of a product lifecycle, but time series models using multiplicative trends need to pay extra attention that such growth is not seen as fixed but given an opportunity to taper off over time. Multiplicative seasonality more naturally incorporates growth, since the seasonality effects should grow with the scale of demand. Additive seasonality usually applies to more mature products with relatively little growth. We illustrate the difference between a stable time series with additive trend and seasonality and a stable time series with multiplicative trend and seasonality in Figure 5.3. Differentiating between these different functional forms is important for the general state space modeling framework we will discuss in Chapter 6.

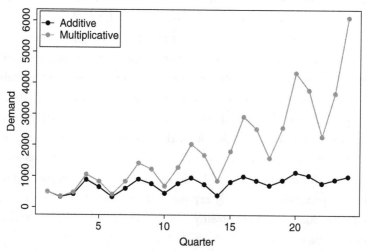

Figure 5.3 Additive and multiplicative trends and seasonality

5.5. Key Takeaways

- In time series decomposition, we separate a series into its seasonal, trend, level, and error components. We analyze these components separately and finally put the pieces back together to create a forecast.
- Components can be decomposed and recombined additively or multiplicatively.
- The challenge of time series modeling lies in understanding how much the time series components change over time.
- Multiplicative components lead to increasing growth/decline patterns over time, whereas additive components imply a more linear growth/decline of firms.

PART III
Forecasting Models

CHAPTER 6

Exponential Smoothing

6.1 Change and Noise

One of the most effective and robust methods for time series forecasting is exponential smoothing. This result has been established in the so-called M-competitions, in which more than 20 forecasting methods were compared for their performance across over 3,000 time series from different industries and contexts (Makridakis and Hibon 2000). The good news is that exponential smoothing is not only an effective, versatile, and robust method but is also, at its core, intuitive and easy to understand and interpret. Another important aspect of the method is that the data storage and computational requirements for exponential smoothing are minimal, and the method can thus be applied with ease to a large number of time series in real time. The theoretical work on exponential smoothing is by now extensive; it can be shown that this method is the optimal one (i.e., one minimizing squared forecast errors) for random walks with noise and a variety of other models of time series (Chatfield et al. 2001; Gardner 2006).

To illustrate how exponential smoothing works, we begin with a simple time series without trend and seasonality. In such a series, variance in demand from period to period is driven either by random changes to the level (i.e., long-term shocks to the time series) or by random noise (i.e., short-term shocks to the time series). The essential forecasting task then becomes estimating the level of the series in each time period and using that level as a forecast for the next period. The key to effectively estimate the level in each period is to differentiate level changes from random noise (i.e., long-term shocks from short-term shocks). As discussed in Chapter 5, if we believe that there are no random-level changes in the time series (i.e., the series is stable), then our best estimate of the level involves using all of our available data by calculating a long-run average over the whole time series. If we believe that there is no random noise in the series (i.e., we can observe the level), our estimate of the level is simply the most recent observation, discounting everything that happens further in the past. Not surprisingly then, the "right" thing to do in a time series that contains both random-level changes and random noise is something in-between these two extremes—that is, calculate a weighted average over all available data, with weights decreasing the further we go back in time. This approach to forecasting, in essence, is exponential smoothing.

Formally, let the index t describe the time period of a time series. The level estimate (=Level) in each period t according to exponential smoothing is then given by the following equation:

$$\text{Level}_t = \text{Level}_{t-1} + \alpha \times \text{Forecast Error}_t \qquad (1)$$

In this equation, the coefficient alpha (α) is a smoothing parameter and lies somewhere between 0 and 1 (we will pick up the topic on what value to choose for α later in this chapter). The Forecast Error in period t is simply the difference between the actual demand (=Demand) in period t and the forecast made for time period t.

$$\text{Forecast Error}_t = \text{Demand}_t - \text{Forecast}_t \qquad (2)$$

In other words, exponential smoothing follows the simple logic of feedback and response. The forecaster derives an estimate of the current level of the time series, which he/she uses as the forecast. This forecast is then compared to the actual demand in the series in the next period, and the level estimate is revised according to the discrepancy between the forecast and actual demand. The forecast for the next time period is then simply equivalent to the current level estimate, since we assumed a time series without trend and seasonality, that is:

$$\text{Forecast}_{t+1} = \text{Level}_t \qquad (3)$$

Substituting equations (2) and (3) into equation (1), we obtain

$$\text{Level}_t = \text{Forecast}_t + \alpha \times \left(\text{Demand}_t - \text{Forecast}_t\right)$$
$$= \left(1 - \alpha\right) \times \text{Forecast}_t + \alpha \times \text{Demand}_t \qquad (4)$$

Exponential smoothing can therefore also be interpreted as a weighted average between our previous forecasts and the currently observed demand.

Curious readers have probably noticed that the method suffers from a "chicken-or-egg" problem: Creating an exponential smoothing forecast requires a previous forecast, which naturally creates the question of how to generate the first forecast. The method needs to be initialized with an appropriate value for the very first forecast. Different initializations are possible, ranging from the very first demand data point over an average of the first few demands to the overall average demand.

With a bit more replacement, equation (4) can in turn be converted into a weighted average over all past demand observations, where the weight of a demand observation that is i time periods away from the present is given as follows:

$$\text{Weight}_i = \alpha \times (1 - \alpha)^i \qquad (5)$$

Equation (5) implies an exponential decay in the weight attached to a particular demand observation the further this observation lies in the past. This is the reason why the technique is referred to as "exponential" smoothing. Figure 6.1 shows the weights assigned to past demand observations for typical values of α. We see that higher values of α yield weight curves that drop faster as we go into the past. That is, the more recent past is weighted higher compared to the more distant past if α is higher. Thus, forecasts will be more adaptive to changes in the market for higher values of α. We further discuss how to set the value of α below.

Forecasts created through exponential smoothing can thus be thought of as a weighted average of all past demand data, where the weight associated with each demand decays exponentially the more distant a demand observation is from the present. It is important, though, that one does not actually have to calculate a weighted average over all past demand in order to apply exponential smoothing; as long as a forecaster consistently follows equation (1), all that is needed is a memory of the most recent forecast and an observation of actual demand to update the level estimate. For that reason, the data storage and retrieval requirements for exponential smoothing are comparatively low. Consistently applying the method simply generates forecasts as if in each period one would calculate

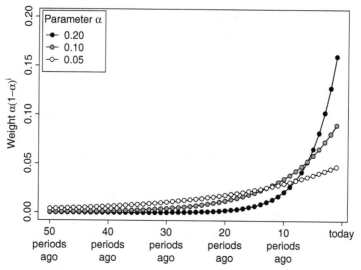

Figure 6.1 *Weights for past demand under exponential smoothing*

a weighted average over all past demand with exponentially decaying weights, as shown in Figure 6.1.

A technique that is sometimes used as an alternative to single exponential smoothing is moving averages. In a moving average of size n, the most recent n demand observations are averaged with equal weights to create a forecast for the future. This method is in essence similar to calculating a weighted average over all past demand observations, with the most recent n observations receiving equal weights and all other observations receiving zero weight. While this method is easy to understand, it naturally leads to the question why there should be such a step change in weighing past demands; that is, while under exponential smoothing all past demand observations receive some weight[1] (just decaying the more you move into the past), moving averages assign equal weights for a while and then no weight at all to the history of demand.

6.2.   Optimal Smoothing Parameters

The choice of the "right" smoothing parameter α in exponential smoothing is certainly important. Conceptually, a high α corresponds to a belief

---

[1]Note that the weight assigned under exponential smoothing to a period in the distant past can become very small (particularly with a high α) but remains positive nonetheless.

that variation in the time series is mostly due to random-level changes; a low α corresponds to a belief that this variation in the series is mostly due to random noise. Consider equation (4) for α = 1. In this special case, which is the highest α possible, the level estimate in each period is equivalent to the currently observed demand, which means that one believes that the time series follows a pure random walk, such as series 2 in Figure 5.2. Conversely, consider equation (5) for α close to 0. In this case, the weight attached to each demand observation in the past is essentially the same, and exponential smoothing corresponds to calculating a long-run unweighted average. This would be the right thing to do for a stable time series such as series 1 in Figure 5.2. Choosing the right α thus corresponds to choosing the type of time series that a focal time series resembles more; series that look more like series 1 should receive a higher α; series that look more like series 2 should receive a lower α. In practice, forecasters do not need to make this choice, but can rely on optimization procedures that will fit exponential smoothing models to past data, minimizing the discrepancy between hypothetical past forecasts and actual past demand observations by changing the α. The output of this optimization is a good smoothing parameter to use for forecasting and can be interpreted as a measure of how much the demand environment in the past has changed over time. High values of α mean that the market was very volatile and constantly changing, whereas low values of α imply a relatively stable market with little persistent change.

6.3   Extensions

One can extend the logic of exponential smoothing to more complex time series. Take, for example, a time series with an (additive) trend and no seasonality. In this case, one proceeds with updating the level estimate in accordance with equation (1), but then additionally estimates the trend in time period t as follows:

$$\text{Trend}_t = \left(1 - \beta\right) \times \text{Trend}_{t-1} + \beta \times \left(\text{Level}_t - \text{Level}_{t-1}\right) \quad (6)$$

This method is also referred to as "Holt's method." Notice the similarity between equations (4) and (6). In equation (6), beta (β) is another smoothing parameter that captures the degree to which a forecaster believes that the trend of a time series is changing. A high β would indicate a trend that can rapidly change over time, and a low β would correspond to a more or less stable trend. We again need to initialize the trend component to start the forecasting method, for example, by taking the difference between the first two demands or the average trend over the entire demand history. Given that we assumed an additive trend, the resulting one-period-ahead forecast is then given by

$$\text{Forecast}_{t+1} = \text{Level}_t + \text{Trend}_t \tag{7}$$

Usually, forecasters do not only need to predict one period ahead into the future, but longer forecasting horizons are a necessity for successful planning. In production planning, for example, the required forecast horizon is given by the maximum lead time among all suppliers for a product—often as far out as 6 to 8 months. Exponential smoothing easily extends to forecasts further into the future as well; for example, in this case of a model with additive trend and no seasonality, the h-step-ahead forecast into the future is calculated as follows:

$$\text{Forecast}_{t+h} = \text{Level}_t + h \times \text{Trend}_t \tag{8}$$

This discussion requires emphasizing an important insight and common mistake for those not versed in applying forecasting methods: Estimates are only updated if new information is available. Thus, the same level and trend estimates are used to project the one-step-ahead and two-step-ahead forecasts at time period t. One cannot, in a meaningful way, update level or trend estimates after making the one-step-ahead forecast and before making the two-step-ahead forecast. In the extreme, in smoothing models without a trend or seasonality, this means that all forecasts for future periods are the same; that is, if we expect the time series to be a "level only" time series without a trend or seasonality, we estimate the level once, and that estimate becomes our best guess for what demand looks like in all future periods. Of course, we understand that this forecast will become worse and worse the more we project into the future owing to the potential instability of the time series (which is a topic we have explored already in Chapter 3), but this expectation does not change the fact that we cannot derive a better estimate for what happens further out in the future at the current time. After observing the next time period, new data becomes available, and we can again update our estimates of the level and thus our forecasts for the future. Thus, the two-step-ahead forecast made in period t (for period $t+2$) is usually different from the one-step-ahead forecast made in period $t+1$ (for period $t+2$).

We note that our trended exponential smoothing forecast extrapolates trends indefinitely. This aspect of the method could be unrealistic for long-range forecasts. For instance, if we detect a negative (downward) trend, extrapolating this trend out will yield negative demand forecasts at some point in the future. Or assume that we are forecasting market penetration and find an upward trend—in this case, if we forecast out far enough, we will get forecasts of market penetration above 100 percent. Thus, trended forecasts should always be truncated appropriately. In addition, few processes grow without bounds, and it is often better to *dampen* the trend component as we project it out into the future. Such trend dampening will not make a big difference for short-range forecasting, but will have a strong impact on long-range forecasting (Gardner and McKenzie 1985).

Similar extensions allow exponential smoothing to apply to time series with seasonality as well. Seasonality parameters are estimated separately from the trend and level components, and an additional smoothing parameter γ (gamma) is used to reflect the degree of confidence a forecaster has that the seasonality in the time series remains stable over time. Such an exponential smoothing approach, with additive trend and seasonality, is often referred to as Holt-Winters exponential smoothing.

The parameter estimation of exponential smoothing models can be unduly influenced if the sample used for fitting the smoothing model includes outlier data. Fortunately, these data problems are by now well understood, and good solutions exist that allow forecasters to automatically prefilter and replace unusual observations in the dataset before estimating smoothing model parameters (Gelper, Fried, and Croux 2010).

In summary, exponential smoothing can be generalized to many different forms of time series. A priori, it is sometimes not clear which exponential smoothing model to use; however, one can essentially run a forecasting competition to figure out which model works best on past data (see Chapter 12). In this context, the innovation state space framework for exponential smoothing is sometimes applied (Hyndman et al. 2008).

One can think of five different variants of trends in time series (none, additive, additive dampened, multiplicative, multiplicative dampened) and three different variants of seasonality (none, additive, multiplicative). Further, one can conceptualize random errors in two different variants (additive, multiplicative). As a result, there are 5 × 3 × 2 = 30 different versions of exponential smoothing possible; this is sometimes referred to as Pegels' classification, and the formulas for applying the exponential smoothing logic in each of these versions are well known (www.otexts.org/fpp/7/7; Gardner 2006). To make this framework work, one can define a hold-out sample (subportion) of the data available, fit each of these 30 models to the data *not* in the hold-out sample, and finally forecast using each separate model into the hold-out period. One then selects the model from this competition that provides the best fit to the data in the hold-out sample, together with the exponential smoothing parameters that generates this best fit, and applies this estimated model to generate forecasts. This application of exponential smoothing seems to be a current gold standard for pure time series forecasting methods and performs very well in general forecasting competitions (Hyndman 2002). A publicly available program that allows using this approach in Excel is available through the add-on PEERForecaster (http://peerforecaster.com/). Similarly, forecasters using the statistical software R can install a free package called "forecast" implementing this forecasting framework as well.

6.4.   Key Takeaways

- Exponential smoothing is a simple and surprisingly effective forecasting technique. It can model trend and seasonality components.
- Exponential smoothing can be interpreted as feedback-response learning, as a weighted average between most recent forecast and demand, or as a weighted average of all past demand observations with exponentially declining weights. All three interpretations are equivalent.
- Your software will usually determine the optimal exponential smoothing model as well as the smoothing parameters automatically. High parameters imply that components are

changing quickly over time; low parameters imply relatively stable components.

- Trends will be extrapolated indefinitely. Consider dampening trends for long-range forecasts. Do not include trends in your model unless you have solid evidence that a trend exists.
- There are up to 30 different forms of exponential smoothing models; modern software will usually select which of these works the best in a time series using a hold-out sample.

CHAPTER 7

ARIMA Models

Besides exponential smoothing, another approach for analyzing time series is the so-called ARIMA, or Box–Jenkins models. ARIMA stands for "Autoregressive Integrated Moving Average." These models are very popular, particularly among econometric forecasters. As we will see later in this chapter, ARIMA models can be seen as a generalization of exponential smoothing models. The popularity of ARIMA models is often explained by the logic that if exponential smoothing models are a special case of ARIMA models, then ARIMA models should outperform, or at least perform equivalent to, exponential smoothing. Unfortunately though, this logic does not seem to hold in reality. In large forecasting competitions (Makridakis 1993b; Makridakis and Hibon 2000), exponential smoothing models regularly beat ARIMA models in out-of-sample comparisons. Nevertheless, ARIMA models are still used in practice, and this chapter will briefly explore the mechanics of ARIMA time series modeling.

7.1   Autoregression

The first component of an ARIMA model is the autoregressive (AR) component. Autoregression means that we conceptualize current demand as being a function of previous demand. This is a slightly different (though mathematically somewhat similar) conceptualization of demand compared to exponential smoothing, where we saw demand as being driven by a constantly changing underlying but unobserved level of the time series. Specifically, if we see demand as driven by only the most recent demand, we can write the simplest form of an ARIMA model, also called an AR(1) model, as follows:

$$\text{Demand}_t = a_0 + a_1 \times \text{Demand}_{t+1} + \text{Error}_t \qquad (9)$$

Equation (9) looks like a regression equation (see Chapter 8), with current demand being the dependent variable and previous demand being the independent variable. This is, in fact, how an AR(1) model is estimated—simply as a regression equation between previous and current demand. One can, of course, easily extend this and add additional terms to reflect a dependency of the time series that goes deeper into the past. For example, an AR(2) model would look as follows:

$$\text{Demand}_t = a_0 + a_1 \times \text{Demand}_{t-1} + a_2 \times \text{Demand}_{t-2} + \text{Error}_t \quad (10)$$

Estimating this model again follows a similar regression logic. In general, an AR(p) model is a regression model that predicts current demand with the p most recent past demand observations.

Trends in a time series are usually "filtered out" before an AR model is estimated by first-differencing the data. Further, it is straightforward to deal with seasonality in this context of AR models. One way of dealing with seasonality would be to deseasonalize data before analyzing a time series, for instance, by taking year-over-year differences. There is also an alternative to such preprocessing by simply including an appropriate demand term in the model equation. Suppose, for example, we examine a time series of monthly data with expected seasonality. We could model this seasonality by allowing current demand to be influenced by demand from 12 time periods ago. In the case of an AR(1) model with seasonality, we would write this specification as follows:

$$\text{Demand}_t = a_0 + a_1 \times \text{Demand}_{t-1} + a_2 \times \text{Demand}_{t-12} + \text{Error}_t \quad (11)$$

7.2   Integration

The next component of an ARIMA model is the "I," which stands for the order of integration. Integration refers to taking differences of demand data prior to analysis. For example, an AR(1)I(1) model would look as follows:

$$\text{Demand}_t - \text{Demand}_{t-1} = a_0 + a_1$$
$$\times \left(\text{Demand}_{t-1} - \text{Demand}_{t-2} \right) + \text{Error}_t \qquad (12)$$

To make things simple, the Greek letter Delta (Δ) is often used to indicate first differences. For example, one can write

$$\Delta\text{Demand}_t = \text{Demand}_t - \text{Demand}_{t-1} \qquad (13)$$

Substituting equation (13) into equation (12) then leads to the following simplified form:

$$\Delta\text{Demand}_t = a_0 + a_1 \times \Delta\text{Demand}_{t-1} + \text{Error}_t \qquad (14)$$

Taking first differences essentially means that, instead of examining demand directly, one analyzes changes in demand. As we have discussed in Chapter 4, this technique is employed to make the time series stationary before running a statistical model. This idea can be extended further. For example, an AR(1)I(2) model uses second differences by analyzing

$$\Delta^2\text{Demand}_t = \Delta\text{Demand}_t - \Delta\text{Demand}_{t-1} \qquad (15)$$

which is akin to analyzing changes in the change in demand instead of demand itself.

To see how a time series becomes stationary through integration, consider the following example of a simple time series with a trend:

$$\text{Demand}_t = a_0 + a_1 \times t + \text{Error}_t \qquad (16)$$

This time series is not stationary, since the mean of the series constantly changes by a factor a_1 in each time period. If, however, we examine the first difference of the time series instead, we observe that in this case

$$\Delta\text{Demand}_t = \left(a_0 - a_0\right)+\left(a_1 \times t - a_1 \times \left(t-1\right)\right)+\left(\text{Error}_t - \text{Error}_{t-1}\right)$$
$$= a_1 + \text{Error}_t - \text{Error}_{t-1} \qquad (17)$$

The two error terms in equation (17) are simply the difference of two random variables, which again is just a random variable in itself. In other words, first differencing turned the time series from a nonstationary series into a stationary one. This effect is illustrated in Figure 7.1. The left part of the figure shows a nonstationary time series with a positive trend. The right hand side of the figure shows the first difference of the same demand observations. Clearly, these first differences now represent noise around a mean, thus making the series of first differences stationary.

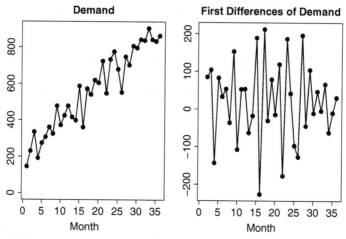

Figure 7.1 *First differencing a time series*

Sometimes (though rarely), the process of first-order differencing is not enough to make a time series stationary, and second- or third-order differencing is needed. Further, some time series require taking the natural logarithm first (which can lead to a more constant variance of the series) or deseaonalizing the series. In practice, many manipulations can be used to achieve stationarity of the series, but differencing represents a very common transformation to achieve this objective.

One can of course argue that all these data manipulations distract from the actual objective. In the end, forecasting is about predicting the next demand in a series, and not about predicting the next first difference in demand. But notice that data manipulations such as first differencing can easily by reversed ex post. Suppose you have used an AR(1)I(1) model to predict the next first difference in demand (= Predicted ΔD_{t+1}). Since you know the currently observed demand, you can simply construct a forecast for demand in period $t+1$ by calculating

$$\text{Forecast}_{t+1} = \text{Predicted } \Delta D_{t+1} + \text{Demand}_t \qquad (18)$$

7.3   Moving Averages

This concludes the discussion of the "I" component of ARIMA models; what remains is to discuss the moving averages (MA) component. Note that this MA component in ARIMA models should not be confused with the MA forecasting method discussed in Section 6.1. This component simply represents an alternative conceptualization of serial dependence in a time series—but this time, the next demand does not depend on the previous *demand* but on the previous *error*, that is, the difference between what the model would have predicted and what we have actually observed. An MA(1) model can be represented as follows:

$$\text{Demand}_t = a_0 + a_1 \times \text{Error}_{t-1} + \text{Error}_t \qquad (19)$$

In other words, instead of seeing current demand as a function of previous demand, we conceptualize demand as a function of previous forecast errors. The difference between AR and MA models, as we shall see later this chapter, essentially boils down to a difference in how persistent random shocks are to the series. Whereas random shocks tend to "linger" for a long time in AR models, they more quickly disappear in MA models. MA models, however, are more difficult to estimate than AR models. While an AR model estimation is very similar to a standard regression, MA models have a bit of a "chicken-or–egg" problem: one has to create an initial error term to estimate the model, and all future error terms will directly depend on what that initial error term is. For that reason, MA models require estimation with more complex maximum likelihood procedures instead of the regular regression we can use for AR models.

MA models extend in a similar fashion as AR models do. An MA(2) model would see current demand as a function of the past two model errors, and an MA(q) model sees demand as a function of the past q model errors. More generally, when combining these components, one can see an ARIMA(p, d, q) model as a model that looks at demand that has been differenced d times, where this dth demand difference is seen as a function of the previous p (dth) demand differences and q forecast errors. Quite obviously, this is a very generic model for demand forecasting, and selecting the right model among this basically infinite set of possible models becomes a key challenge. One could apply a "brute force" technique, as in exponential smoothing, and simply examine which model among a wide range of choices fits best in an estimation sample. Yet, unlike in exponential smoothing, where the number of possible models was limited, there is a nearly unlimited number of models available here, since one could always go further into the past to extend the model. The next subsection will show how to use the autocorrelation function (ACF) to select a good ARIMA model.

7.4   Autocorrelation and Partial Autocorrelation

Two tools used in practice for identifying an adequate ARIMA model are the so-called autocorrelation function (ACF) and partial autocorrelation functions (PACF). For the ACF, one calculates the sample correlation (= CORREL function in Excel) between the current demand and the previous demand, between the current demand and the demand before the previous demand, and so on. By going n time periods into the past, this leads to n correlation coefficients between current demand and the demand lagged by n time periods. These correlations are called "autocorrelations," because they describe the correlation of demand with itself ("auto" in Greek meaning "self"). Autocorrelations are usually plotted against lag order in a bar plot, the so-called "autocorrelation plot." Figure 7.2 contains an example of such a plot. One frequently also sees horizontal lines in such an autocorrelation plot, which differentiate autocorrelations that are statistically significant from nonsignificant ones, that is, autocorrelation estimates that are higher (or lower, in the case of negative autocorrelations) than we would expect by chance. This can help in identifying the orders p and q of an ARIMA model.

The partial ACF works similar by estimating first an AR(1) model, then an AR(2) model, and so on, and always recording the regression coefficients of the last term that is added to the equation. To illustrate how to calculate the ACF and the PACF, consider the following example. Suppose we have a demand time series, and calculate the correlation coefficient between demand in a current period and the time period before ($r_1 = 0.84$), as well as the correlation coefficient between demand in a current period and demand in the time period before the previous one ($r_2 = 0.76$). The first two entries of the ACF are then 0.84 and 0.76. Suppose now that we additionally estimate two regression equations:

$$\text{Demand}_t = \text{Constant} + \theta_{1,1}\,\text{Demand}_{t-1} + \text{Error}_t$$
$$\text{Demand}_t = \text{Constant} + \theta_{2,1}\,\text{Demand}_{t-1} + \theta_{2,2}\,\text{Demand}_{t-2} + \text{Error}_t \quad (20)$$

Suppose that the results from this estimation show that $\theta_{1,1} = 0.87$ and $\theta_{2,2} = 0.22$. The first two entries of the PACF are then 0.87 and 0.22.

The ACF can be used to differentiate MA(1) and AR(1) processes from each other, as well as differentiate both of these processes from demand which represents simple draws from a distribution without any serial dependence. To illustrate this selection process, Figure 7.2 contains the time series and ACF plots of a series following an AR(1) process, an

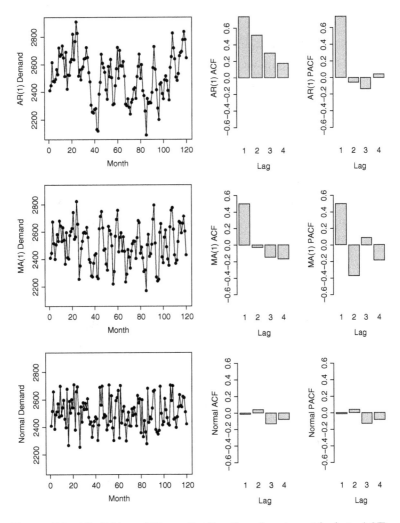

Figure 7.2 **AR, MA and Normally distributed series with their ACF and PACF**

MA(1) process, and data which represents simple draws from a normal distribution. Note that all three series were generated using the same random draws to enhance comparability. One can see that the MA(1) series and the normal series look very similar; only a comparison of their ACFs reveals that while the normally distributed demand shows no autocorrelation in any time lag, the MA(1) series shows an autocorrelation going back one time period (but no further). The AR(1) process, however, looks very distinct in comparison. Shocks from the series tend to throw the series off from the long run average for longer periods of time. In other words, if demand drops, it will likely stay below average for some time before it recovers. This distinctive pattern is clearly visible in the ACF for the AR(1) process; the autocorrelation coefficients in the series are present in all four time lags depicted, though they slowly decrease as the time lag increases.

7.5   Discussion

One can show that using single exponential smoothing as a forecasting method is essentially equivalent to using an ARIMA(0,1,1) model as a forecasting method. With optimal parameters, the two series of forecasts produced will be the same. The logical conclusion is then that since ARIMA(0,1,1) models are a special case of ARIMA(p, d, q) models, ARIMA models represent a generalization of exponential smoothing and thus must be more effective at forecasting.

While this logic is compelling, it has not withstood empirical tests. Large forecasting competitions have repeatedly demonstrated that exponential smoothing models tend to dominate ARIMA models in out-of-sample comparisons (Makridakis and Hibon 2000). It seems that exponential smoothing is simply more robust. Further, with the more general state space modeling framework, the variety of exponential smoothing models has been extended such that many of these models are not simply special cases of ARIMA modeling anymore. Thus, ARIMA modeling is not necessarily preferred anymore as a forecasting method in general; nevertheless, the use of these models continues to enjoy some popularity. ARIMA modeling is recommended "for a series showing short-term correlation where the variation is not dominated by trend and seasonality, provided the forecaster has the technical expertise to understand how to carry out the method" (Chatfield 2007). If ARIMA models are used as a forecasting method, one usually does not need to consider a high differencing order. Most series can be well modeled with no more than two differences (i.e., $d \leq 2$) and AR/MA terms up to order five (i.e., $p, q \leq 5$) (Ali et al. 2015).

While ARIMA models focus on point forecasts, a similar class of models, called GARCH (generalized autoregressive conditional heteroscedasticity) focuses on modeling the uncertainty inherent in forecasts as a function of previous shocks (i.e., forecast errors). These models are often employed in stock market applications and stem from the observation that large shocks to the market in one period create more volatility in succeeding periods. The key to these models is to view the variance of forecast errors not as fixed, but as a function of previous errors, effectively creating a relationship between previous shocks to the time series and future uncertainty of forecasts. GARCH can be combined with ARIMA models since the former technique is focused at modeling the variance of a distribution while the latter models the mean. A good introduction to GARCH modeling is given in Engle (2001) and Batchelor (2010).

7.6   Key Takeaways

- ARIMA models explain time series based on autocorrelation, integration, and moving averages. They can be applied to time series with seasonality and trend.
- These models have not performed particularly well in demand forecasting competitions, but they are included in most forecasting software packages.
- Your software should identify the best differencing, AR, and MA orders automatically, as well as estimate the actual AR and MA coefficients. If not, ACF and PACF plots can be used to identify AR and MA orders.
- You will typically not need high AR, MA or differencing orders for the model to work.

CHAPTER 8

Causal Models and Leading Indicators

8.1 Leading Indicators

The time series forecasting methods discussed in the previous two chapters have one key advantage: the only data they require are the time series data themselves; no additional data are needed to estimate a smoothing parameter, or the parameters of an ARIMA model, and use it for forecasting. However, firms often have a range of additional information available that could be used to create demand forecasts as well, such as consumer confidence indices, advertising projections, reservations made or orders already placed, and so forth. Using such information falls into the domain of *causal modeling* and *leading indicators*.

A useful leading indicator is given by additional data that is available (or predictable) in advance, not prohibitively costly to obtain, and that improves forecasting performance when used in a forecasting model. Of course, the cost of obtaining such data has to be judged in comparison to the improvement in forecasting performance that will result from using it. An important point here is that the leading indicator needs to provide more information than what is contained in the time series already; leading indicators are often subject to the same seasonal effects than a focal time series, and simple correlations between leading indicators and the focal series can be a result of their joint seasonality. A key to a successful evaluation of the performance of leading indicators is not simply to demonstrate a correlation between the leading indicator and your demand time series but also to show that using the leading indicator in forecasting improves upon forecasts when used in addition to the time series itself.

In order to use leading indicators for forecasting, we need to know or be able to forecast their values for the future. We may be able to forecast advertising budgets rather well. Conversely, assume that we wish to forecast the sales of a weather-sensitive product like garden furniture or ice cream. If the weather is nice and sunny, we will sell more than if it is rainy and wet. However, if we want to use weather information to improve forecasts, we will need to feed the *forecasted* weather into our causal forecast algorithm, and of course the question is then whether we can forecast the weather sufficiently well far enough into the future to improve on sales forecasts that do not use the weather. Of course, we are assuming that the obvious seasonality is already included in our "weather-less" forecasts.

To illustrate the use of leading indicators, consider a dataset on sales and advertising. The dataset contains 3 years of monthly data on sales as well as advertising expenses during the month for a dietary weight control product (Abraham and Ledolter 1983). A time series plot of the dataset is given in Figure 8.1. One could apply some form of exponential smoothing to the sales data to create a forecast—or one could attempt to use advertising expenses to predict sales. An easy way to examine whether advertising expenses explain higher sales is to calculate the correlation coefficient

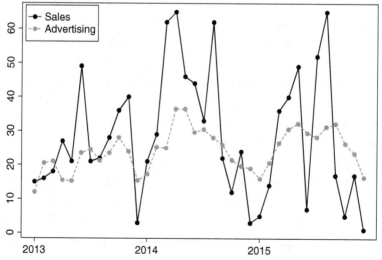

Figure 8.1 *Time series on sales and advertising*

between these variables. In Microsoft Excel, this can be easily done using the = CORREL function. In this case, the correlation between the two measures is $r = 0.63$, which is statistically significant; this would indicate that, from a statistical perspective, advertising expenses relate to sales.

So is advertising a useful leading indicator? The first question would be whether the advertising expenses for a month are actually known in advance. Usually, the advertising budgets are set according to some plan, so many firms will know their advertising expenses for a future month in advance. However, the time lag with which this information is available then effectively determines the forecast horizon that can be achieved. If advertising expenses are known only 1 month in advance, they can only be used for 1-month-ahead predictions.

A related discussion would be whether there is a time lag between spending money on advertising and these expenses having any influence on sales; in this case, one can check for a possible time lag involved by comparing the correlation between sales and current advertising expenses ($r = 0.63$) to the correlation between sales and last month's advertising expenses ($r = 0.30$), or even the expenses from 1 month earlier ($r = 0.34$). Clearly the correlation is strongest with the current advertising expenses, indicating that a time lag is probably not a major worry for forecasting. Some drivers of demand can also influence multiple time periods. Promotions, for example, clearly influence demand for the period in which they happen, but some of that extra demand due to the promotion in a period may simply be shifted demand from the time period succeeding the promotion.

Another discussion one can have is whether the underlying relationship is actually causal. One could, for example, argue for reverse-causality (i.e., it is not advertising that is driving sales, but sales that is driving advertising) or alternative explanations (i.e., if companies advertise, they also stock more product, leading to higher service levels and sales). These questions are empirically hard to resolve, although much progress has been made in recent years in econometrics to better address questions of causality, and interested readers are referred to Angrist and Pischke (2009) for a good overview of these methods.

It is essential to emphasize that forecasting does not require a causal relationship; forecasting is, in that sense, a very pragmatic profession. As long as data enable us to predict the future better, we do not need to be certain that the underlying relationship is truly causal. While we can have more confidence that the relationship we use for forecasting remains stable over time if we understand the underlying causality, being unable to demonstrate causality does not necessarily prevent us from exploiting an empirical relationship to make predictions. In other words, if we know that a statistical relationship exists between the number of storks in a country and the birthrate of a country ($r = 0.62$; see Matthews 2000), can we use this relationship to predict the birth rate of a country for which we have counted only the number of storks but know nothing else about? The answer is yes (assuming we can forecast the number of storks well enough). In the absence of other data, exploiting this relationship may be the best we can do. However, questioning causality may lead us to better predictors. In this case, the number of storks in a country relates to country size, which in turn relates to birth rates. Using country size will probably lead to better predictions of births than using the number of storks.

In this context, "big data" is providing forecasters with new opportunities to find leading indicators that help in the prediction of their time series. Google, for example, provides two tools available for free: Google Trends and Google Correlate (Choi and Varian 2012). Google Trends allows forecasters to examine the frequency of certain search terms relative to all searches over time. Google Correlate provides the functionality to upload your own time series and then examine which search terms correlate the most with your uploaded time series. A recent example focusing on end-consumer personal consumption expenses in different categories shows how incorporating this information into standard forecasting methods can lead to large increases in forecasting accuracy (Schmidt and Vosen 2013). Note, however, that while Google Trends offers current data, Google Correlate only comes with a time lag of up to 6 months. In that sense, Google Correlate offers a tool to identify possible search terms that may become viable leading indicators, and Google Trends allows downloading and using this data for forecasting in real time.

8.2   Combination With Time Series

Going back to our advertising and sales data from the previous section, the key question to answer is how much we actually gain by using the advertising data, that is, how much better we can predict sales if we exploit the relationship between advertising and sales, as opposed to simply using the time series history of sales to predict the future. To answer this question, we devise a forecasting competition (see Chapter 12) by splitting the dataset at hand into an estimation sample (years 1–2) and a hold-out sample (year 3). The estimation sample is used to estimate the relationship between advertising and sales; the hold-out sample is used to test the predictions of that model. Specifically, we will calculate a *rolling origin forecast*. That is, we take the history from January 2013 to December 2014, fit a model, and forecast for January 2015. Next, we move the forecast origin by 1 month, taking the history from January 2013 to January 2015, fitting a model and forecasting for February 2015, and so forth. In each step, we estimate the following regression equation using data from the first months:

$$\text{Sales}_t = a_0 + a_1 \times \text{Advertising}_t + \text{Error}_t \qquad (21)$$

Estimating a regression equation here essentially means finding values of a_0 and a_1 that minimize the squared values of Error$_t$ across the estimation sample. Interested readers who require more background on the topic of regression are referred to a different book by the same publisher (Richardson 2011). A regression equation can be estimated in Excel if the data analysis tool pack is installed. A free add-in for Excel that allows for more detailed analysis is available at http://regressit.com/. In our case, in the first step, we estimate the equation to obtain the following estimates for a_0 and a_1:

$$\text{Sales}_t = -15.92 + 1.97 \times \text{Advertising}_t + \text{Error}_t \qquad (22)$$

These estimates indicate that for prediction purposes, every dollar spent in advertising is associated with $1.97 in extra sales on average. It becomes important to emphasize that this is not necessarily a causal effect, and these numbers should not be used to plan advertising spending; however, if we know what the advertising budget is, we can multiply that number with 1.97 (and subtract 15.92) to create a prediction of sales in that period. In the second step, we have one additional historical data point, so our estimated model changes slightly:

$$\text{Sales}_t = -18.14 + 2.05 \times \text{Advertising}_t + \text{Error}_t \qquad (23)$$

This rolling regression approach is easy to do for all 12 months in the hold-out sample (i.e., year 33) and leads to a mean absolute error (MAE; see Chapter 11 on forecast error measures) of 15.07 across the hold-out sample. How good is this forecast? A reasonable comparison is a pure time series forecast that would not have required any information on advertising. To that purpose, we estimated exponential smoothing forecasts (as described in Chapter 4), again using rolling forecasts. The winning models across our 12 forecast origins generally were models with additive or multiplicative errors, without trends or seasonality. The resulting MAE from these model forecasts is 22.03, higher than the MAE from our simple regression model.

We can see from Figure 8.2 that the two sets of forecasts are very different. Which forecast should one trust? The MAE from exponential smoothing models is higher. But does that mean that one should rely solely on the advertising data? Or can these two methods somehow be combined to provide better forecasts? One way to combine time series models with leading indicators is to allow for the regression equation to estimate seasonal factors (and/or trends). Since trends played little role in our data, we will ignore them for now. To incorporate seasonality into the regression equation, we code 11 "dummy" variables in our dataset, one for each month except for December. A code of "1" indicates that a particular observation in the dataset takes place in that particular month; the variables are 0 otherwise. If all variables are coded as "0" for an observation, that observation took place in December.[1] We then estimate the following multivariate regression equation:

$$\text{Sales}_t = a_0 + a_1 \times \text{Advertising}_t + a_2 \times \text{January} + \ldots + a_{12}$$
$$\times \text{November} + \text{Error}_t \qquad (24)$$

---

[1] In general, a categorical variable with N categories requires $N-1$ dummy variables to represent in a regression equation, since the absence of all other categories indicates the presence of the omitted category. If N dummy variables are used instead (in addition to a regression intercept), these variables become perfectly correlated as a set, and estimating the regression equation will not be possible.

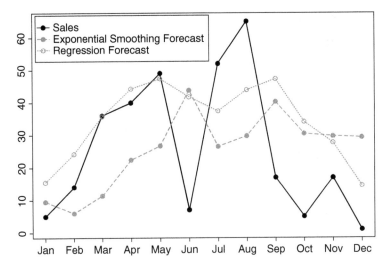

Figure 8.2 Rolling regression and exponential smoothing forecasts in the hold-out sample

This equation now accounts for seasonality according to different months. However, the way seasonality is included limits the effects of seasonality to be additive in nature and does not allow the seasonality effects to change over time. We calculated forecasts for the hold-out samples using this revised specification. The resulting MAE (=15.84) is worse than in the original model, indicating that incorporating seasonality in this fashion was not beneficial. Is there possibly a better way of combining time series information with advertising information to create a better forecast? The correlation between forecast errors from the exponential smoothing model and advertising expenses for that month in the hold-out sample is 0.41; while this could simply be due to randomness, since statistical significance is hard to show in such small samples, it gives us some indication that advertising may contain relevant information that is not captured by the sales time series alone.

This question of forecasting with multiple methods has been studied extensively in the literature on forecast combination, and there is much evidence that combining forecasts from different methods provides superior forecasts (Armstrong 2001). In our case, we could simply take the average of the exponential smoothing and the regression forecast. While such a strategy often works to improve performance, in our case, the resulting

MAE is not improved (=17.53). In general, if a time series is very unstable, using the simple average instead of some optimal weight seems appropriate (Armstrong and Collopy 1998) and should be considered as an option to combine forecasts from multiple methods.

8.3   Key Takeaways

- Known drivers of demand can dramatically improve your forecast. Consider including them in a causal model.
- It is not sufficient to demonstrate that a driver correlates with demand; rather, for the driver to be useful in forecasting, the forecasting performance improvement that can be obtained by using the demand driver, compared to simple time series models without the driver, needs to outweigh the cost of obtaining the necessary data.
- A driver's influence on demand may lag behind its occurrence and may influence more than a single time period.
- For forecasting demands with a causal driver, we need to measure and forecast the driver. An unforecastable driver, like the specific weather on a day 3 months ahead, is useless.
- Regression models with leading indicators can be combined with time series models to create better forecasts.

CHAPTER 9

Count Data and Intermittent Demands

9.1 Definitions

So far, we have focused on using the normal distribution for forecasting. Using the normal distribution can be inappropriate for two reasons: First, the normal distribution is *continuous*, that is, a normally distributed random variable can take noninteger values, like 2.43. Second, the normal distribution is *unbounded*, that is, a normally distributed random variable can take negative as well as positive values. Both these properties of the normal distribution do not make sense for (most) demand time series. Demand is usually integer-valued, apart from products sold by weight or volume, and demand is usually zero or positive, but not negative, apart from returns.

These seem pretty obvious ways in which the normal distribution deviates from reality. So why do we nevertheless use this distribution? The answer is simple and pragmatic: *because it works*. On the one hand, using the normal distribution makes the statistical calculations that go on "under the hood" of your statistical software (optimizing smoothing parameters, estimating ARIMA coefficients, calculating prediction distributions) much easier. On the other hand, the actual difference between the forecasts—both point and distribution—under a normal or a more appropriate distribution is often small, especially for fast-moving products. However, this volume argument to support using the normal distribution does not hold any more for slow-moving demand time series.

Now, we can address both problems explained above by using *count data distributions*, which are random number distributions that only yield integer values. Common distributions to model demands are the Poisson

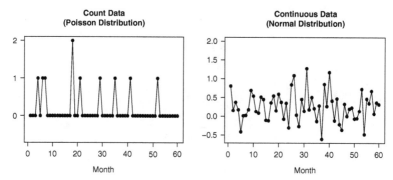

Figure 9.1 Random draws for count data and continuous data for low-volume products

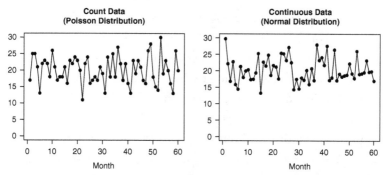

Figure 9.2 Random draws for count data and continuous data for high-volume products

and the negative binomial distribution (Syntetos et al. 2011). The Poisson distribution has a single parameter that is both its mean and variance. The more flexible negative binomial distribution has one parameter for the mean and another one for its variance.[1]

Figure 9.1 illustrates the difference between Poisson-distributed demands and normally distributed "demands," at a common rate of 0.2 units per month. We see both problems discussed above (negative and noninteger demands) in the normally distributed data, whereas the Poisson time series does not exhibit such issues and therefore appears more realistic. Conversely, Figure 9.2 shows that there is little difference between

---

[1]Technically, the extra parameter of the negative binomial distribution captures overdispersion, that is, the amount by which the variance of the distribution exceeds its mean.

a Poisson and a normal distribution for fast-moving products—here, at a rate of 20 units per month.

Once demand gets so slow that many time buckets in fact exhibit zero demand, we speak of *intermittent* demand series. We will use the terms "count data" and "intermittent demand" interchangeably. Finally, there is *lumpy demand*. Demand is "lumpy" if it is intermittent *and* nonzero demands are high. Lumpy demand can occur, for instance, for upstream supply chain members who have only a few customers that place batch orders, or in home improvement retail or wholesale stores, where house builders will typically buy large quantities of a particular paving stone or light switch at once. Low-volume intermittent data is often the result of many customers placing orders rarely; high-volume lumpy demand results from a few customers aggregating their orders into large batches. We illustrate the differences and similarities between these concepts in Figure 9.3.

Why is it important to forecast intermittent or lumpy demand? We naturally focus on forecasting the fastest moving products, simply because these products have the highest visibility in the firm (and market) and are often the most important ones in terms of margin and total revenue. However, most businesses also have a "Long Tail" of slow-moving products. By the anecdotal Pareto principle, 80 percent of your SKUs will be responsible for 20 percent of your sales. Classic A-B-C analysis in inventory management naturally differentiates between these fast- and slow-moving items. Many from these 80 percent of SKUs probably have intermittent demand series. While it is important to improve the forecasts for the 20 percent fast-movers that drive 80 percent of sales, the many

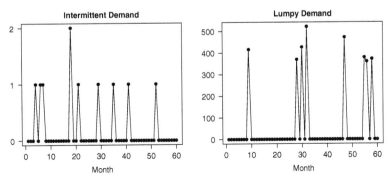

Figure 9.3 *Intermittent and lumpy demand series. Note vertical axes*

more slow-movers may represent a much larger fraction of your total inventory value. Accurate forecasts can help you reduce these inventories, pool them, move to a make-to-order process, or improve your operations in other ways. There may actually be as large an improvement opportunity here as there is for faster moving items.

In addition, the occurrence of intermittent time series is often driven by several recent developments. A few years ago, database capacity and processing power limited the number of demand time series to be stored and forecasted on a weekly basis. Nowadays, vastly more powerful storage and processing (Januschowski et al. 2013) allow working with ever-lower granularity. And a time series that is fast-moving on a weekly basis may well be slow moving on a daily basis and can be heavily intermittent on an hourly basis. The more a firm disaggregates the time unit used for forecasting, the more likely the firm is to encounter intermittent data. Further, a small product portfolio which slices a market into only a few segments by providing a few different variants will likely produce high-volume series. However, with more and more product differentiation, many variants themselves may become intermittent in demand. Thus, due to increased product variety as well as data storage capacity available, we will see and need to forecast more and more intermittent time series in the future.

9.2   Traditional Forecasting Methods

Given the particularities of intermittent demand, how should we forecast series with such count data? Could we use the methods described in the previous three chapters in this context as well? We apply single exponential smoothing with a smoothing parameter of $\alpha = 0.10$ (as per Chapter 6) to an intermittent demand series in Figure 9.4.

Remember that single exponential smoothing creates forecasts by calculating a weighted average between the most recent forecast and the most recent demand. Thus, the forecasts tend to drop and slowly move toward zero over time when no demand is observed. However, after demand is observed, forecasts briefly "jump" up again. Thus, our forecast is high right after a nonzero demand and low after a long string of zero demands.

This form of forecasting does not make sense in two important situations. First, consider a context where our intermittent demand is driven

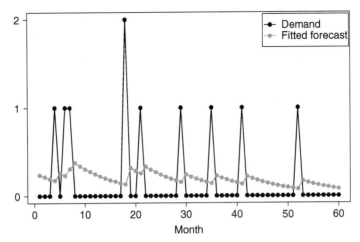

Figure 9.4 Single exponential smoothing applied to an intermittent time series

by a few customers that replenish this SKU when they need it; in this case, we would need a higher forecast (and not a lower forecast) after a long string of zero demands, because it becomes *more* likely that these customers will place an order again as more time passes. Second, if we have a context where the intermittent demand is driven by many customers buying independently, the forecast should not exhibit any time dynamics at all, because at any point in time, there is an equally large pool of customers that may soon demand the product. In addition, we will typically make replenishment or production decisions right after our stock has been depleted by a sale, so forecasts that are biased high right after sales will lead to particularly high reorder quantities and to unnecessarily high inventories. To overcome these problems, we will focus our attention now on a method that is designed to overcome these challenges.

9.3   Croston's Method

Croston (1972) examines the problem of forecasting intermittent demand and proposed a specific solution to this problem. This solution is by now an industry standard and bears Croston's name. Instead of exponentially smoothing the raw demands, we separately smooth two different time series: (1) all the nonzero demands from the original time series and (2) the number of periods with zero demands between each instance of nonzero demand. In a sense, we decompose the forecasting problem into the subproblems of predicting how frequently demand happens and predicting how high the demand is if it happens. We highlight the values associated with these two time series in Figure 9.5.

Thus, the problem becomes one of forecasting the series of nonzero demands, that is, {1, 1, 1, 2, 1, 1, 1, 1, 1}, and the series of time periods in-between nonzero demands, that is, {1, 0, 10, 2, 7, 5, 5, 10} in Figure 9.5. Croston's method essentially applies exponential smoothing to both these series (usually with the same smoothing parameters). Further, we only update the two exponential smoothing forecasts for these two series whenever we observe a nonzero demand.

Let us assume that smoothing the nonzero demands yields a forecast of q, while smoothing the numbers of zero demand periods yields a forecast of r. This means that we forecast nonzero demands to be q, while we expect such a nonzero demand once every r periods on average. Then, the demand point forecast in each period is simply the ratio between these two forecasts, that is,

$$Forecast = q \:/\: r \tag{25}$$

Croston's method works through averages; while the method is not designed to predict *when* a particular demand spike occurs, it essentially

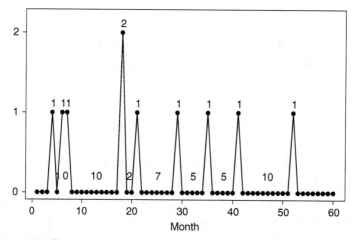

Figure 9.5 *Demand and time periods without demand in an intermittent series*

distributes the volume of the predicted next demand spikes over the time periods expected until that demand spike occurs. One could also think of Croston's method as predicting the ordering behavior of a single client with fixed ordering costs. According to the classic Economic Order Quantity model, a downstream supply chain partner will lump continuous demand into order batches in order to balance the fixed cost of order/shipping with the variable cost of holding inventory; Croston's method could then be seen as a way of predicting the demand this downstream supply chain partner sees—that is, to remove the order variability amplification caused by batch ordering from the time series. Figure 9.6 provides an example of how Croston's method forecasts an intermittent demand series.

Croston's method provides some temporal stability of forecasts but does not address the problem that, for a small number of customers, long periods of nonordering should indicate a higher likelihood of an order being placed. Further, Croston's method works by averaging and forecasting the *rate* at which demand comes in, not by predicting when demand spikes occur; this makes it hard to interpret forecasts resulting from Croston's method for decision making. The forecast may say that, *on average* over the next 5 weeks, we will sell one unit each week—where, in fact, there is likely only 1 week during which we sell five units.

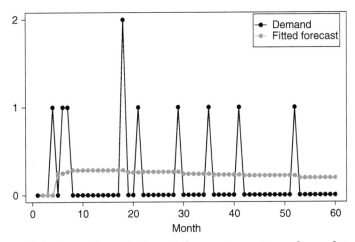

Figure 9.6 Croston's method applied to an intermittent demand time series

As a matter of fact, a closer theoretical inspection shows that Croston's method suffers from a statistical bias (Syntetos and Boylan 2001). Technically, this bias occurs because equation (24) involves taking expectations of random variables, and we approximate the expectation of a ratio between nonzero demands and interdemand intervals by the ratio of the expectations. Various correction factors to compensate for this problem have been proposed and implemented in modern forecasting software. One example of such a correction procedure is the Syntetos-Boylan approximation (Syntetos and Boylan 2005; Teunter and Sani 2009), which has been found to often lead to better inventory positions (Syntetos, Babai, and Gardner 2015).

Croston's method is very simple and may appear to be "too simple." Why is it nevertheless very often used in practice? One factor is of course its simplicity—it can be quickly explained, and the logic underlying the method is intuitive to understand. Another explanation may be that intermittent demand often does not exhibit a lot of dynamics that can reasonably be modeled: it is very hard to detect seasonality—trends or similar effects in intermittent demands—so it usually does not make sense to try to create a better model. In fact, competing models for intermittent demands have been proposed, but their added complexity needs to be weighed against any gain in accuracy compared to Croston's method—and no other method has so far consistently outperformed Croston's method with the Syntetos-Boylan approximation.

That said, there is one situation in intermittent demand forecasting where Croston's method does not perform very well, namely, for lumpy demands. Suppose we have a demand of one unit once in every 10 weeks (nonlumpy demand), or of 10 units once in every 100 weeks (lumpy demand). Average demand is $1/10 = 10/100 = 0.1$ unit per week in both cases. Croston's method will yield forecasts of about this magnitude in both cases. However, the two cases have very different implications for inventory holding. This is really not a shortcoming of Croston's method as such, because a point forecast of 0.1 is a completely correct summary of the long-run average demand. The problem lies in the fact that the point forecast does not consider the *spread* around the average. Unfortunately, there is no commonly accepted method for forecasting lumpy demands for inventory control purposes. Most forecasters use an ad hoc method like "stock up to the highest historical demand," use a standard forecasting method with high safety stocks, or try to reduce their reliance on forecasting for such time series by managing demand and moving to a make-to-order system as much as possible. The challenges of intermittent demand forecasting are one reason why spare parts inventory systems (which generally have intermittent demand patterns) are more and more utilizing additive manufacturing to print spare parts on demand (D'Aveni 2015).

9.4   Key Takeaways

- Count data and intermittent demands are probably responsible for only 20 percent of your sales, but may account for 80 percent of your inventory costs. Therefore, it makes sense to invest into forecasting them well.
- Do not use exponential smoothing or ARIMA to forecast intermittent demands. Instead, use Croston's method or other methods that are dedicated to intermittent series.
- If you can expand the time unit being analyzed or aggregate across locations, you can often convert intermittent time series into nonintermittent series that are easier to forecast.
- Lumpy demands are particularly hard to forecast, since the average rate may be useless for inventory control.

CHAPTER 10

Human Judgment

10.1 Intuition vs. Cognition

Any visit to the business book section of a local bookstore will reveal plenty of titles that emphasize that managers need to trust their gut feeling and follow their instincts (e.g., Robinson 2006), indicating that their judgment should play an essential role in organizational decision-making processes. The last three decades of academic research have, however, also produced a counter-movement to this view, which mostly centers on the study of cognitive biases (Kahneman, Lovallo, and Sibony 2011). In this line of thought, human judgment is seen as inherently fallible. Intuition, as a decision-making system, has evolved in order to help us quickly make sense of the surrounding world, but its purpose is not necessarily to process all available data and carefully weigh alternatives. Managers can easily fall into the trap of trusting their initial feeling and thereby biasing decisions, rather than carefully deliberating and reviewing all available data and alternatives. A key for effective human judgment in forecasting is to be able to reflect upon initial impressions and to let further reasoning and information possibly overturn one's initial gut feeling (Moritz, Siemsen, and Kremer 2014).

The presence of cognitive biases in time series forecasting is well documented. In particular, forecasters tend to be strongly influenced by recent data in a series, and they neglect to interpret this recent data in the context of the whole time series that has created it. This pattern is also called system neglect (Kremer, Moritz, and Siemsen 2011). It implies that forecasters tend to overreact to short-term shocks in the market and underreact to real and massive long-term shifts. Further, forecasters are easily misled by visualized data to "spot" illusionary trends. Simple random walks (such as stock market data) have a high likelihood of creating sequences of observations that seem to consistently increase or decrease over time by pure chance. This mirage of a trend is quickly seen as a real trend, even if the past series provides little indication that actual trends exist in the data. Using such illusionary trends for prediction can be highly misleading. Finally, if actual trends do exist in the data, human decision makers tend to dampen these trends as they extrapolate in the future; that is, their longer range forecasts tend to exhibit a belief that these trends are temporary in nature and will naturally degrade over time (Lawrence and Makridakis 1989). Such behavior may be beneficial for long-term forecasts where trends usually require dampening, but may decrease performance for more short-term forecasts.

This discussion also enables us to point out another important judgment bias in the context of time series. Consider series 1 in Figure 5.2. As mentioned earlier, the best forecast for this series is a long-run average of observed demand. Thus, plotting forecasts for multiple future periods would result in a flat line—the forecast would remain the same from month to month. A comparison of the actual demand series with the series of forecasts made reveals an odd picture; the demand series shows considerable variation, whereas the series of forecasts is essentially a straight line. Human decision makers tend to perceive this as odd and thus introduce variation into their series of forecasts, so that the series of forecasts more resembles the series of actual demands (Harvey, Ewart, and West 1997). Such behavior is often called "demand chasing" and can be quite detrimental to forecasting performance.

Another important set of biases relates to how people deal with the uncertainty inherent in forecasts. One key finding in this context is overprecision—human forecasters tend to underestimate the uncertainty in their own forecasts (Mannes and Moore 2013). This bias likely stems from a tendency to ignore or discount extreme cases. The result is that prediction intervals that are based on human judgment tend to be too narrow—people feel too precise about their predictions. While this bias has been very persistent and difficult to remove, recent research in this area has provided some promising results by showing that overconfidence can be reduced if decision makers are forced to assign probabilities to extreme outcomes as well (Haran, Moore, and Morewedge 2010). A related bias is the so-called hindsight bias. Here, decision makers tend to believe ex post that their forecasts are more accurate than they actually are (Biais and Weber 2009). This highlights the importance of constantly calculating, communicating, and learning from the accuracy of past judgmental forecasts.

Thus, while cognitive biases relate more generally to organizational decision making, they are also very relevant in our context of demand forecasting. However, to see judgment as only biased is a limited perspective. Statistical algorithms do not know what they do not know, and human judgment may have domain specific knowledge that enables better forecasting performance than any algorithm can achieve. Recent research shows that, with the proper avenues of decision making, the forecasting performance of human judgment can be extraordinary (Tetlock and Gardner 2015).

10.2   Domain-Specific Knowledge

One important reason why human judgment is still prevalent in organizational forecasting processes is the role of domain-specific knowledge in forecasting (Lawrence, O'Connor, and Edmundson 2000). Human forecasters may have information about the market that is not (or only imperfectly) incorporated into their current forecasting models, or the information is too difficult to quantify that it cannot be included in forecasting models. Such information in turn enables them to create better forecasts than any statistical forecasting model could accomplish. From this perspective, the underlying forecasting models appear incomplete. Key variables that influence demand are not included in the forecasting models used. In practice, forecasters will often note that their models do not adequately factor in promotions, which is why their judgment is necessary to adjust any statistical model. Yet, in modern times of business analytics, such arguments seem more and more outdated. Promotions are quantifiable in terms of discount, length, advertisement, and so forth. Good statistical models to incorporate such promotions into sales forecasts are now available (e.g., Cooper et al. 1999) and have been successfully applied in practice.

Besides incompleteness, forecasters may have noncodifiable information, that is, a highly tacit and personal understanding of the market.

Sales people may, for example, be able to subjectively assess and interpret the mood of their customers during their interactions and incorporate such information into their forecasts. They may also get an idea of the customers' own estimate of how their business is developing, even if no formal forecast information is shared. The presence of such information hints at model incompleteness as well, yet, unlike promotions, some of this information may be difficult to quantify and include in any forecasting model.

Another argument in favor of human judgment in forecasting is that such judgment can be apt at identifying interactions among predictor variables (Seifert et al. 2015). An interaction effect means that the effect of one particular variable on demand depends on the presence (or absence) of another variable. While human judgment is quite good at discerning such interaction effects, identifying the right interactions can be a daunting task for any statistical model, due to the underlying dimensionality. The number of possible j-way interaction terms among k variables is given by the binomial of k over j. For example, the possible number of two-way interactions among 10 variables is $9 + 8 + 7 + \ldots + 2 + 1 = 45$; the possible number of three-way interactions among 10 variables in a regression equation is 120. Including that many interaction terms in a regression equation can make the estimation and interpretation of any statistical model very challenging. Human judgment may be able to preselect meaningful interactions more easily.

The presence of domain-specific knowledge among forecasters overall is a valid argument why human judgment should play a role in organizational forecasting processes. There are, however, also arguments that may explain the presence of human judgment in such processes as well, but do not point to clear performance advantages of human judgment. One such argument is the "black box" argument: Statistical models are often difficult to understand for human decision makers; thus, they trust the method less and are more likely to discount it. In laboratory experiments, the users of forecasting software were more likely to accept the forecast from the software if they could select the model to be used from a number of alternatives (Lawrence, Goodwin, and Fildes 2002), and they tend to be more likely to discount a forecast if the source of the forecast is indicated as a statistical model as opposed to a human decision maker (Önkal et al. 2009). Quite interestingly, human decision makers tend to forgive other human experts that make errors in forecasts, but quickly lose their trust in an algorithm that makes prediction errors (Dietvorst, Simmons, and Massey 2015). Due to the noise inherent in time series, both humans and algorithms will make prediction errors eventually, yet over time, this implies that algorithms will be less trusted than humans. However, if we think about it, whether the user understands and trusts a statistical model does not, by itself, mean that the model yields bad forecasts! Since we care about the accuracy of our forecasts, not the popularity of our model, the "black box" argument, by itself, should not influence us against a statistical model. Another and potentially more damaging argument is the presence of political concerns around the forecast.

10.3   Political and Incentive Aspects

Dividing firms into functional silos is often a necessary aspect of organizational design to achieve focus in decision making. Such divisions usually go hand-in-hand with incentives—marketing and sales employees may, for example, be paid a bonus depending on the realized sales of a product, whereas operations employees may be provided with incentives based on costs. The precise key performance indicators used vary significantly from firm to firm. While such incentives may provide an impetus for action and effort within the corresponding functions, they necessarily create differing organizational objectives within the firm. Such differing objectives are particularly troublesome for cross-functional processes such as forecasting and sales and operations planning.

Since the forecast is a key input for many organizational decisions, decision makers try to influence the forecast to achieve their organizational objectives. Sales people could, for example, attempt to *inflate* the forecast in order to influence their manufacturing counterparts to provide more available inventory, or they may *reduce* the forecast in order to overachieve sales and get a big bonus; representatives from the finance department may alter the forecast so that it conforms more with how they want to represent the company and its prospects to investors; operations may again inflate the forecast to increase their safety margin (instead of cleanly identifying a safety stock). Relying on a statistical model will eliminate the ability to influence decision making through the forecast; as such, any organizational change in that direction will encounter resistance.

A recent article provides a fascinating description of seven different ways of how ineffective processes can lead forecasters to play games with their forecasts (Mello 2009). *Enforcing* behavior occurs when forecasters try to maintain a higher forecast than they actually anticipate, with the purpose of reducing the discrepancy between forecasts and company financial goals. If senior management creates a climate where goals simply have to be met, forecasters may acquiesce and adjust their forecasts accordingly to reduce any dissonance between their forecasts and these goals. *Filtering* occurs when forecasters lower their forecasts to reflect supply or capacity limitations. This often occurs if these forecasts are driven by operations personnel that will use the opportunity to mask their inability to meet the actual predicted demand. If forecasts are strongly influenced by sales personnel, *hedging* can occur, where forecasts overestimate demand in order to drive operations to make more products available. A similar strategy can occur if forecasts are influenced by downstream supply chain partners that anticipate a supply shortage and want to secure a larger proportion of the resulting allocation.[1] On the contrary, *sandbagging* involves lowering the sales forecast so that actual demand is likely to exceed it; this strategy becomes prevalent if forecasts and sales targets are not effectively differentiated within the organization. *Second guessing* occurs when powerful individuals in the forecasting process override the forecast with their own judgment. This is often a symptom of general mistrust in the forecast or the process that delivered it. The game of *spinning* occurs if lower-level employees or managers deliberately alter (usually increase) the forecast in order to influence the responses of higher-level managers. This is a result of higher-level management "killing the messenger". That is, if forecasters get criticized for delivering forecasts that are low, they will adjust their behavior to deliver "more pleasant" forecasts instead. Finally, *withholding* occurs when members of the organization fail to share critical

---

[1]Note that such order gaming behavior can be avoided by using a uniform instead of a proportional allocation rule by the supplying company (Cachon and Lariviere 1999). With uniform allocation, limited supply is equally divided among all customers; if a customer receives more supply than he/she ordered, the excess units are allocated equally among the remaining customers.

information related to the forecast. This is often a deliberate ploy to create uncertainty about demand among other members in the organization.

In summary, there are good and bad reasons why human judgment is used in modern forecasting processes. The question of whether its presence improves forecasting is ultimately an empirical one. In practice, most companies will use a statistical forecast as a basis for their discussion, but often adjust this forecast based on the consensus of the people involved. Forecasting is ultimately a statement about reality, and thus the quality of a forecast can be easily judged ex post (see Chapter 11). One can thus compare over time whether the adjustments made in this consensus adjustment process actually improved or decreased the accuracy of the initial statistical forecast, which has been called a "Forecast Value Added" analysis (Gilliland 2013). In a study of over 60,000 forecasts across four different companies, such a comparison revealed that, on average, judgmental adjustments to the statistical forecast increased accuracy (Fildes et al. 2009). However, a more detailed look also revealed that smaller adjustments (which were more frequent) tended to decrease performance, whereas larger adjustments increased performance. One interpretation of this result is that larger adjustments were usually based on model incompleteness, that is, promotions and foreseeable events that the statistical model did not consider. The smaller adjustments represent the remaining organizational quibbling, influencing behavior and distrust in the forecasting software. One can thus conclude that a good forecasting process should only be influenced by human judgment in exceptional circumstances and with clear indication that the underlying model is incomplete; organizations are otherwise well advised to limit the influence of human judgment in the process.

10.4   Correction and Combination

If judgmental forecasts are used in addition to statistical forecasts, two methods exist that may help to improve the performance of these judgmental forecasts: combination and correction. Combination methods simply combine judgmental forecasts with statistical forecasts in a mechanical way as described at the end of Chapter 8. In other words, the simple average of two forecasts—whether judgmental or statistical—can outperform either one (Clemen 1989).

Correction methods, on the other hand, attempt to de-bias a judgmental forecast before use. Theil's correction method is one such attempt, and it follows a simple procedure. A forecaster starts by running a simple regression between his/her past forecasts and past demand in the following form:

$$\text{Demand}_t = a_0 + a_1 \times \text{Forecast}_t + \text{Error}_t \qquad (26)$$

Results from this regression equation are then used to de-bias all forecasts made after this estimation by calculating

$$\text{Corrected Forecast}_{t+n} = a_0 + a_1 \times \text{Forecast}_{t+n} \qquad (27)$$

where a_0 and a_1 in equation (27) are the estimated regression intercept and slope parameters from equation (26). There is some evidence that this method works well in de-biasing judgmental forecasts and leads to better performance of such forecasts (Goodwin 2000). However, the cautionary warning would be to examine whether the sources of bias change over time. For example, the biases human forecasters experience when forecasting a time series for the first time may be very different from the biases they are subject to with more experience in forecasting the series; thus, initial data may not be valid for the estimation of equation (26). Further, if forecasters know that their forecasts will be bias-corrected in this fashion, they may show a behavioral response to overcome and outsmart this correction mechanism.

The essence of forecast combination methods has also been discussed in the so-called Wisdom of Crowds literature (Surowiecki 2004). The key observation in this line of research is more than 100 years old: Francis Galton, a British polymath and statistician, famously observed that during bull-weighing competitions at county fairs (where fairgoers would judge the weight of a bull), individual estimates could be far off the actual weight of the bull, but the average of all estimates was spot on and even outperformed the estimates of bull-weighing experts. In general, estimates provided by groups of individuals tended to be closer to the true value than estimates provided by individuals. An academic debate ensued whether this phenomenon was either due to group decision making, that is, groups being able to identify the more accurate opinions through discussion, or due to statistical aggregation, that is, group decisions representing a consensus that was far from the extreme opinions within the group, thus canceling out error. Decades of research established that the latter explanation is more likely to apply. In fact, group consensus processes to discuss forecasts can be highly dysfunctional because of underlying group pressure and other behavioral phenomena. Group decision-making processes that limit the dysfunctionality inherent in group decision making, such as the Delphi method and the nominal group technique, exist, but the benefits of such methods for decision making in forecasting compared to simple averaging are not clear. In fact, the simple average of opinions seems to work well (Larrick and Soll 2006). Further, the average of experts in a field is not necessarily better than the average of amateurs (Surowiecki 2004). In other words, decision makers in forecasting are often well advised to skip the process of group meetings to find a consensus; rather, they should prepare their forecasts independently. The final consensus can then be established by a simple or weighted average of these independent forecasts. The random error inherent in human judgment can thus be effectively filtered out. The benefit of team meetings in forecasting should therefore be more seen in stakeholder management and accountability, than in actually improving the quality of the forecast.

This principle of aggregating independent opinions to create better forecasts is powerful, but also counterintuitive. We have an inherent belief that experts should be better judges, and reaching consensus in teams should create better decisions. The wisdom of crowd argument appears to contradict some of these beliefs, since it implies that seeking consensus in a group may not lead to better outcomes, and that experts can be beaten by a group of amateurs. The latter effect has been recently demonstrated in the context of predictions in the intelligence community (Spiegel 2014). As part of the Good Judgment Project, random individuals from across the United States have been preparing probability judgments on global events. Their pooled predictions often beat the predictions of trained CIA analysts with access to confidential data. If amateurs can beat trained professionals in a context where such professionals clearly have domain knowledge, the power of the wisdom of crowds becomes quite apparent. The implication is that for key forecasts in an organization, having multiple forecasts prepared in parallel (and independently) and then simply taking the average of such forecasts may be a simple yet effective way of increasing judgmental forecasting accuracy.

10.5   Key Takeaways

- Human judgment can improve forecasts, especially if humans possess information that is hard to consider within a statistical forecasting method.
- Cognitive biases imply that human intervention will often make forecasts worse. That a statistical method is hard to understand does not mean that a human forecaster will be able to improve the forecast.
- Incentive structures may reward people to make forecasts worse. People will try to influence the forecast, since they have an interest in influencing the decision that is based on the forecast.
- Measure whether and when human judgment actually improves forecasts. It may make sense to restrict judgmental adjustments to only those contexts where concrete information of model incompleteness is present (e.g., the forecast does not factor in promotions, etc.).
- When relying on human judgment in forecasting, get independent judgments from multiple forecasters and then average these opinions.

PART IV

Forecasting Quality

CHAPTER 11

Forecast Quality Measures

So far we have studied several forecasting algorithms. Most of these can have many different variants, depending on whether seasonality, trend, and so forth are included or not. The question therefore arises how to decide whether one algorithm does a better job at forecasting a given time series than another one—that is, we need to benchmark methods and find those that work the best in our context. We thus need *forecast quality* key performance indices (KPIs), or *error measures.*

Performance measurement is necessary for management; if we do not measure performance, it is hard to set goals and coordinate activities to a purpose. This statement is true for almost any aspect of a business, but particularly so for forecasting. However, it is counter to how society often treats forecasting (Tetlock and Gardner 2015). Pundits on television can make bold statements about the future without their feet being held to the fire; management gurus are praised when one of their predictions has come true, without ever considering their long-run record. A similar culture can exist in organizations—managerial gut judgments are taken as fact, without ever establishing whether the forecaster making the judgment has a history of being spot on, or mostly off. Even worse, forecasts are often made in such a way that it becomes impossible to examine their quality, particularly since the forecast does not include a proper time frame; the good news is that in demand forecasting, forecasts are usually quantified ("we expect demand for SKU X to be Y") and come with a time frame ("Z months from now"). Such a specificity allows explicitly calculating the error in the forecast and thus making long-run assessments of this error. Unfortunately, despite these benefits of quantification, it still turns out that deciding whether a demand forecast is "good" or whether one forecasting algorithm is "better" than another is not completely straightforward—which is why we will devote this chapter to the topic.

11.1   Bias and Accuracy

The aim of this section is to introduce the concepts of *bias* and *accuracy* in forecast error measurement and to provide an overview of commonly used metrics for this purpose. Suppose we have calculated a single point forecast $\hat{y}$ and later on observe the corresponding demand realization y. We will define the corresponding error as

$$e = \hat{y} - y \qquad (28)$$

For instance, if $\hat{y} = 10$ and $y = 8$, then $e = 10 - 8 = 2$. This definition has the advantage that overforecasts (i.e., $\hat{y} > y$) correspond to *positive* errors, while underforecasts (i.e., $\hat{y} < y$) correspond to *negative* errors, in accordance with everyday intuition. Note that, with a slight rearrangement, this definition means that

$$y = \hat{y} - e \qquad (29)$$

or "actuals equal the model *minus* the error," instead of "*plus*," which is a common convention in modeling sciences such as statistics or machine learning, where one would define the error as $e = y - \hat{y}$. Such a definition would yield the unintuitive fact that overforecasts (or underforecasts) would correspond to negative (or positive) errors.

As a matter of fact, our error definition, although common, is not universally accepted in forecasting research and practice, and many forecasters adopt the alternative error definition motivated by statistics and machine learning. Green and Tashman (2008) conducted a survey among practicing forecasters as to their favorite error definition and offered some additional commentary. Even our own definition of forecast error in Chapter 6 defines the error in its alternate form—mostly because this alternative definition makes exponential smoothing easier to explain and understand.

Whichever convention you adopt in your practical forecasting work, the key takeaway is that whenever you discuss errors, you need to make sure everyone is using the *same* definition. Note that this challenge does not arise if the only thing we are interested in are *absolute* errors.

Demand forecasts cannot be judged in their quality unless a sufficient number of forecasts have been made. As discussed in Chapter 1, if we examine just a single forecast error, we have no means of differentiating between bad luck and a bad forecasting method. Thus, we will not calculate the error of a single forecast and realization, but instead calculate errors of many forecasts made by the same method. Let us assume that we have n forecasts $\hat{y}_1, \ldots, \hat{y}_n$ and n corresponding actual realizations y_1, $\ldots, y_n$, giving rise to n errors, that is,

$$e_1 = \hat{y}_1 - y_1, \ldots, e_n = \hat{y}_n - y_n \qquad (30)$$

Our task is to summarize this (potentially very large) number of errors in a way that we can make sense of it. The simplest way of summarizing a large number of errors is to take its average. The *mean error* (ME) is the simple average of errors,

$$ME = \tfrac{1}{n} \sum e_i \qquad (31)$$

The ME tells us whether a forecast is "on average" on target. This is the key metric used to assess bias in a forecasting method. If ME = 0, then the forecast is on average *unbiased*, but if ME > 0, then we systematically overforecast demand, and if ME < 0, then we systematically underforecast demand. In either case, if ME ≠ 0 and the distance between ME and 0 is sufficiently large, we say that our forecast is *biased*.

While the notion of bias is an important one, quite often we are less interested in *bias* than in the *accuracy* of a forecasting method. While bias measures whether on average a forecast is on target, accuracy measures how close the forecast is to actual demand, on average. In other words, while the bias examines the mean of the forecast error distribution, the accuracy relates to the spread of the forecast error distribution. One often used metric to assess accuracy is the *absolute* difference between a point forecast $\hat{y}$ and the corresponding realization y, that is,

$$|e| = |\hat{y} - y| \qquad (32)$$

where |.| means that we take the value between the "absolute bars," that is, dropping any plus or minus sign. Thus, the absolute error cannot be negative. For instance, if the actual realization is $y = 8$, then a forecast of $\hat{y} = 10$ and one of $\hat{y} = 6$ would both be two units away from the actual in either direction, and the absolute error is 2 for either forecast. The *mean absolute error* (MAE) or *mean absolute deviation* (MAD)—both terms are used interchangeably—is the simple average of *absolute errors*,

$$MAE = MAD = \frac{1}{n}\sum |e_i| \tag{33}$$

Note here that we need to take absolute values *before* and not after summing the errors. For instance, assume that $n = 2$, $e_1 = 2$, and $e_2 = -2$. Then $|e_1| + |e_2| = |2| + |-2| = 2 + 2 = 4 \neq 0 = |2 + (-2)| = |e_1 + e_2|$. The MAE tells us whether a forecast is "on average" *accurate*, that is, whether it is "close to" or "far away from" the actual, without taking the sign of the error into account.

Let us consider an artificial example (cf. Figure 11.1). Assume that our point forecast is $\hat{y} = (11, 11, \ldots, 11)$, that is, we have a constant forecast of 11 for $n = 10$ months. Assume further that the actual observations are $y = (10, 12, 10, 12, 10, 12, 10, 12, 10, 12)$. Then the errors are $e = (1, -1, 1, -1, 1, -1, 1, -1, 1, -1)$ and ME = 0, that is, our flat forecast is unbiased. However, it is not very accurate, since MAD = 1. Conversely, assume that the forecast is $\hat{y} = (9.5, 11.5, 9.5, 11.5, \ldots, 9.5, 11.5)$. In this case, our errors are $e = -(-0.5, -0.5, \ldots, -0.5)$, and every single forecast is 0.5 unit too low. Therefore, ME = -0.5, and our forecasts are biased (more precisely, biased *downward*). However, these forecasts are more accurate than the original ones, since their MAE = 0.5. In other words, even though being unbiased often means that a forecast is more accurate, this relationship is not guaranteed, and forecasters sometimes have to decide whether they prefer a biased but more accurate method over an unbiased but less accurate one.

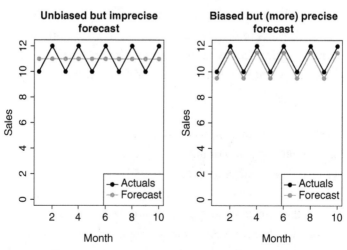

Figure 11.1 Bias vs. accuracy

Which of the two forecasts shown in Figure 11.1 is better? This question cannot be answered in isolation. We usually want our forecasts to be unbiased, since over- and underforecasts cancel out in the long run for unbiased forecasts. This logic would favor the first set of forecasts. However, the second set of forecasts captures the zigzag pattern in the realizations better, at the expense of bias. To decide which forecast is "better," we would need to assess which one leads to better decisions in plans that depend on the forecast, for example, which forecast yields lower stocks and out-of-stocks (which in turn depends, in addition to point forecasts, on accurate estimates of future residual variances and in fact on predictive distributions).

How strong a bias do our error measures need to exhibit to provide us with evidence that a forecasting method actually is biased? After all, it is highly unlikely that the average error is exactly equal to zero. To answer this question, we need to standardize the observed average forecast error by the observed variation in forecast errors—much akin to calculating a test statistic. This is the objective of the tracking signal, which is calculated as follows:

$$TS = \frac{\sum e_i}{MAE} \tag{34}$$

The tracking signal is constantly monitored. If it falls outside certain boundaries, the forecast is deemed biased. A general rule of thumb is that if the tracking signal consistently goes outside to range of ±4, that is, if the running sum of forecast errors is four times the average absolute deviation, then this constitutes evidence that the forecasting method has become biased.

One other very common point forecast accuracy measure, which is often used as an alternative to the MAE, works with *squared* errors, that is, e^2. The square turns every negative number into a positive one, so similar to absolute deviations, squared errors will again always be nonnegative. In order to summarize multiple squared errors $e_1^2, \ldots, e_n^2$, one can calculate the *mean squared error* (MSE),

$$MSE = \tfrac{1}{n} \sum e_i^2 \tag{35}$$

The MSE is another measure of accuracy, not of bias. In the example in the previous section, the first (constant) forecast yields MSE = 1, whereas the second (zigzag) forecast yields MSE = 0.25.

Should one use absolute (i.e., MAE) or squared (i.e., MSE) errors to calculate the accuracy of a method? Squared errors have one important property: Because of the process of squaring numbers, they emphasize large errors much more than absolute errors. Indeed, suppose that in the example above we change a single actual realization from 10 to 20, without changing the forecasts. Then the MEs change a little to -1 and -1.5, the MAEs change slightly to 1.8 and 1.5, but the MSE changes drastically to 9 and 11.25.

Through the process of squaring errors, MSE becomes more sensitive to outlier observations than MAE—which can be a good thing (if outliers are meaningful) or distracting (if you do not want to base your decision making on outlier observations). If you use the MSE, it is always important to screen forecasts and actuals for large errors and to think about what these mean—if these are not important in the larger scheme of things, you may want to remove them from the forecast quality calculation or switch to an absolute error measure instead.

In addition, squared errors have one other technical but very important property: Estimating the parameters of a forecasting model by minimizing the MSE will always lead to unbiased errors, at least if we understand the underlying distribution well enough. The MAE does not have this property—optimizing the MAE may lead to systematically biased forecasts, especially when we forecast intermittent or count data (see Chapter 9 and Morlidge 2015 as well as Kolassa 2016a).

Finally, squared errors and the MSE are expressed in "squared units." If, for example, the forecast and the actual demand are both expressed in dollars, the MSE will be denoted in "squared dollars." This scale is rather unintuitive. One remedy is to take the square root of the MSE, to arrive at the *root mean squared error* (RMSE)—an error measure that is similar to a standard deviation and thus somewhat easier to interpret.

Note that all summary measures of error we considered so far (the ME, MAE/MAD, MSE, and RMSE) have one important weakness: They are not scale-independent. If a forecaster tells you that the MAE associated with forecasting a time series with a particular method is 15, you have no idea how good this number actually is. If average demand in that series is at about 2,000, an MAE of 15 would imply very good forecasts! If, however, the average demand in that series is only 30, then an MAE of 15 would be seen as evidence that it is very difficult to forecast the series. Thus, without knowing the scale of the series, interpreting any of these measures of bias and accuracy is difficult. One can always use them to compare different methods for the same series (i.e., method 1 has an MAE of 15 and method 2 has an MAE of 10 on the same series; thus method 2 seems better), but any comparison between series becomes challenging.

Typically, we will forecast not a single time series but multiple ones, for example, multiple SKUs, possibly in multiple locations. Each time series will be on a different order of magnitude. One SKU may sell tens of units per month, while another one may sell thousands. In such cases, the forecast errors will typically be on similar orders of magnitude—tens of units for the first SKU and thousands of units for the second SKU. Thus, if we use a point forecast quality measure like the MAE to decide, say, between different possible forecast algorithms applied to all series, our result will be completely dominated by the performance of the algorithms on the faster-moving SKU, although the slower-moving one may well be equally or more important. To address this issue, we will try to express all error summaries on a common scale, which we can then meaningfully summarize in turn. For this, we will consider both *percentage* errors and *scaled* errors.

11.2   Percentage and Scaled Errors

To scale forecast errors according to their time series, *percentage* errors express errors as a fraction of the corresponding actual demand realization, that is,

$$p = e \, / \, y = \left(\hat{y} - y \right) / \, y \qquad (36)$$

These percentage errors are often articulated as percentages instead of fractions. Thus, a forecast of $\hat{y} = 10$ and an actual realization of $y = 8$ will yield a percentage error of $p = (10 - 8)/8 = 0.25$, or 25 percent.

As in the case of unscaled errors in the previous subsection, the definition we give for percentage errors in equation (36) is the most common one used, but it is not the only one encountered in practice. Some forecasters prefer to divide the error not by the actual (i.e., y) but by the forecast (i.e., $\hat{y}$; see Green and Tashman 2009). One advantage of this alternative approach is that while the demand can occasionally be zero within the time series (creating a division by zero problem when using demand as a scale), forecasts are less likely to be zero. This modified percentage error otherwise has similar properties as the percentage error defined in equation (36), and the same key takeaway as for "simple" errors applies: all definitions have advantages and disadvantages, and it is most important to agree on a common error measure in a single organization so we do not compare apples and oranges.

Percentage errors $p_1 = e_1/y_1, \ldots, p_n = e_n/y_n$ can be summarized in a similar way as "regular" errors. For instance, the *mean percentage error* is the simple average of p_i,

$$MPE = \frac{1}{n}\sum p_i \tag{37}$$

The MPE plays a similar role to the ME as a measure of "relative" bias. Similarly, we can calculate single *absolute percentage errors* (APEs),

$$APE = |p| = |e / y| = |(\hat{y} - y) / y| = |(\hat{y} - y)| / y \tag{38}$$

where one assumes $y > 0$. APEs can then be summarized by averaging to arrive at the *mean APE* (MAPE),

$$MAPE = \frac{1}{n}\sum |p_i| \tag{39}$$

which is an *extremely* common point forecast accuracy measure.

At this point, let us take a step back and look a little closer at the definition of percentage error. First, note that percentage errors are *asymmetric*. If we exchange the forecast $\hat{y}$ and the actual y, then the error switches its sign, but the absolute error and the squared error do not change at all. In contrast, the percentage error changes in a way that depends on both $\hat{y}$ and y if we exchange the two. For instance, $\hat{y} = 10$ and $y = 8$ yield $p = 0.25 = 25$ percent, but $\hat{y} = 8$ and $y = 10$ yield $p = 0.20 = 20$ percent. The absolute error is 2 and the squared error is 4 in either case. Thus, positive and negative forecast errors are treated differently with percentage error measures. Second, there is another problem here. If $y = 0$, then p entails a division by zero, which is mathematically undefined. If the actual realization is zero, then *any* nonzero error is an infinite fraction or percentage of it. Accordingly, if y becomes very small, p can become very large. There are various ways of dealing with this division by zero problem, some better, some not so good. Let us consider these in turn.

Some forecasting software "deals" with the problem by sweeping it under the rug: in calculating the MAPE, it only sums p_i's whose corresponding y_i's are greater than zero (Hoover 2006). Needless to say, this approach is *not* a good way of addressing the issue. It amounts to positing that we do not care at all about the forecast $\hat{y}_i$ if $y_i = 0$, but if we make production decisions based on the forecast, then it will matter a lot whether prediction was $\hat{y}_i = 100$ or $\hat{y}_i = 1000$ for an actual demand of zero—and such an error should be reflected in the forecast accuracy measure.

An alternative, which also addresses the asymmetry of percentage errors noted above, is to "symmetrize" the percentage errors by dividing the error not by the actual but by the average of the forecast and the actual (Makridakis 1993a), that is,

$$s = \left(\hat{y} - y\right) / \left(\left(\hat{y} + y\right) / 2\right) \tag{40}$$

and then summarizing the absolute values of s_i's as usual, yielding a *symmetric MAPE* (sMAPE),

$$sMAPE = \frac{1}{n}\sum\left|s_i\right| \tag{41}$$

Assuming that at least one of $\hat{y}$ and y are positive, s is well defined, and calculating the sMAPE poses no mathematical problems. In addition, s is symmetric in the sense above: if we exchange $\hat{y}$ and y, then s changes its sign, but its absolute value $|s|$ remains unchanged.

Unfortunately, some *conceptual* problems remain with this error definition as well. In particular, while the sMAPE is symmetric under exchange of forecasts and actuals, it introduces a new kind of asymmetry (Goodwin and Lawton 1999). If the actual realization is $y = 10$, then forecasts of $\hat{y} = 9$ and $\hat{y} = 11$ (an under- and overforecast of one unit, respectively) both result in APEs of $0.10 = 10$ percent. However, $\hat{y} = 9$ yields $|s| = 0.105 = 10.5$ percent, whereas $\hat{y} = 11$ yields $|s| = 0.095 = 9.5$ percent. Generally, an underforecast $\hat{y} = y - \Delta$ by a difference $\Delta > 0$ will yield a larger $|s|$ than an overforecast $\hat{y} = y + \Delta$ by the same amount, whereas the APE will be the same in both cases, $|p| = \Delta/y$.

And this asymmetry is not the last of our worries. As noted above, using s instead of p means that we can mathematically calculate a symmetric percentage error even when $y = 0$. However, what does actually happen for this symmetrized error when $y = 0$? Let us calculate:

$$s = (\hat{y} - y)/([\hat{y} + y]/2) = (\hat{y} - 0)/([\hat{y} + 0]/2) = \hat{y}/(\hat{y}/2) = 2 = 200 \text{ percent.}$$

That is, whenever $y = 0$, the symmetric error s contributes 200 percent to the sMAPE, again completely regardless of the forecast $\hat{y}$ (Boylan and Syntetos 2006). Dealing with zero demand observations in this way is not much better than simply disregarding errors whenever $y = 0$, as above.

Finally, we can calculate a percentage summary of errors in a different way to address the division by zero problem. The *weighted MAPE* (wMAPE) is defined as

$$wMAPE = \sum |e_i| / \sum y_i = MAE / \text{Mean} \qquad (42)$$

A simple computation (Kolassa and Schuetz 2007) shows that we can interpret the wMAPE as a *weighted* average of APEs if all $y_i > 0$, where each APE_i is weighted by the corresponding y_i. That is, in the wMAPE, a given APE has a higher weight if the corresponding realization is larger, which makes intuitive sense. In addition, the wMAPE is mathematically defined even if some $y_i = 0$, as long as not *all* $y_i = 0$.

Now, the interpretation of wMAPE as a weighted average APE, with weights corresponding to actual y_i, immediately suggests alternative weighting schemes. After all, while the actual y_i is one possible measure of the "importance" of one APE, there are other possibilities of assigning an "importance" to an APE, like the cost of an SKU or its margin, or anything else. All these different measures of importance could be used in constructing an alternative wMAPE.

Apart from the problem with dividing by zero, which we can address by using the wMAPE, the APE has another issue, which does not necessarily invalidate its use, but which should be kept in mind. In forecasting demands, we have a natural lower bound of zero, both for actuals and for forecasts. It will (usually) not make sense to forecast $\hat{y} = -10$. Thus, our forecasts and actuals are constrained to $0 \leq \hat{y}, y < \infty$. Now, assume that $y = 10$. Of course, a perfect forecast of $\hat{y} = 10$ yields APE $= |p| = 0$ percent. A forecast of $\hat{y} = 0$ yields APE $= |p| = 1 = 100$ percent, as does a forecast of $\hat{y} = 2 \times y = 20$. However, a forecast of $\hat{y} = 30$ yields APE

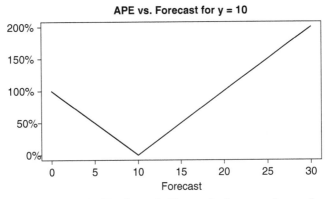

Figure 11.2 The MAPE is bounded by underforecasts but unbounded by overforecasts

= 200 percent. That is, the APE is bounded by 100 percent for underforecasts but unbounded for overforecasts (Figure 11.2).

Thus, the APE is asymmetric as well: A forecast that can be either too high or too low may be penalized more strongly if it turns out to be too high than if it turns out to be too low.

Kolassa and Martin (2011) give a simple illustration of this effect that you can try at home. Take any standard six-sided die and forecast its roll. Assuming the die is not loaded, all six numbers from one to six are equally likely, and the average roll is 3.5. Thus, an unbiased forecast would also be 3.5. What MAPE would we expect from forecasting 3.5 for a series of many die rolls? We can simulate this expected MAPE empirically by rolling a die many times. Alternatively, we can calculate it abstractly, by noting that we have one chance in six in rolling a one, with an APE of $|1-3.5|/1 = 250$ percent, another one-in-six chance of rolling a two, with an APE of $|2-3.5|/2 = 75$ percent, and so on. It turns out that our expected MAPE is 70.97 percent.

We can use our dice to see what happens if we use a biased forecast of 4 instead of an unbiased forecast of 3.5. Little surprise here: the long-run MAPE of a forecast of 4 is worse than for a forecast of 3.5: it is 81.11 percent. However, what happens if our forecast is biased low instead of high? This time, we are in for a surprise: A forecast of 3 yields an expected MAPE of 60.83 percent, clearly lower than the MAPE for an unbiased forecast of 3.5. And an even more biased forecast of 2 yields a yet lower long-run MAPE of 51.67 percent. Try this with your dice at home!

Explaining this effect requires understanding the asymmetry of MAPE. Any forecast higher than 2 will frequently result in an APE that is larger than 100 percent, for example, if we roll a one. Such high APEs pull the average up more than lower APEs can pull it down. The bottom line is that the expected MAPE is minimized by a forecast that is heavily biased downward. Obviously, using this KPI can then lead to very dysfunctional incentives in forecasting.

Interestingly enough, this simple example also shows that alternatives to "plain vanilla" MAPE, such as the sMAPE or the MAPE with the forecast as a denominator, are also minimized by forecasts that differ from the actual long-run average. This asymmetry in the APE creates a perverse incentive to calculate a forecast that is biased low, rather than one that is unbiased but has a chance of exceeding the actual by a factor of 2 or more (resulting in an APE >100 percent). A statistically savvy forecaster might even be tempted to apply a "fudge factor" to the statistical forecasts obtained using his/her software, reducing all system-generated forecasts by 10 percent.

An alternative to using percentage errors is to calculate *scaled* errors, where the MAE/MAD, MSE, or RMSE (or indeed any other nonscaled error measure) are scaled by an appropriate amount. One scaled error measure is *mean absolute scaled error* (MASE; Hyndman and Koehler 2006; Hyndman 2006; Franses 2016). Its computation involves not only forecasts and actual realizations but also *historical* observations used to calculate forecasts. Specifically, assume that we have historical observations $y_1, \ldots, y_T$, from which we calculate one-step-ahead, two-step-ahead, and later forecasts $\hat{y}_{T+1}, \ldots, \hat{y}_{T+h}$, which correspond to actual realizations $y_{T+1}, \ldots, y_{T+h}$. Using this notation, we can write our MAE calculations as follows:

$$MAE = \left(\left| \hat{y}_{T11} - y_{T11} \right| + \cdots + \left| \hat{y}_{T1h} - y_{T1h} \right| \right) / h \qquad (43)$$

Next, we calculate the MAE that would have been observed historically if we had used naïve one-step-ahead forecasts in the past—that is, simply using the previous demand observation as a forecast for the future. The naïve one-step forecast for period 2 is the previous demand y_1, for period 3 the previous demand y_2, and so forth. Specifically, we calculate

$$MAE' = \left(\left| y_1 - y_2 \right| + \ldots + \left| y_{T-1} - y_T \right| \right) / (T - 1) \qquad (44)$$

The MASE then is the ratio of MAE and MAE′:

$$MASE = MAE \ / \ MAE'\ \qquad (45)$$

The MASE scales MAE by MAE′. It expresses whether our "real" forecast error (MAE) is larger than the in-sample naïve one-step-ahead forecast (MASE > 1) or smaller (MASE < 1). Since both numerator and denominator are on the level of the original time series, we can compare the MASE between different time series.

Two points should be kept in mind. First, the MASE is often miscalculated. Correct calculation requires using the *in-sample*, naïve forecast for MAE′, that is, basing the calculations on historical data used to estimate the parameters of a forecasting method. Instead, forecasters often use the *out-of-sample*, naïve forecast to calculate MAE′, that is, the data that the forecasting method is applied to. This miscalculation also results in a scaled quality measure that is comparable between time series and, as such, is quite defensible, but it simply is not "the" MASE as defined in literature.[1] As always, one simply needs to be consistent in calculating, reporting, and comparing errors in an organization.

Second, as discussed above, a MASE > 1 means that our forecasts have a worse MAE than an in-sample, naïve, one-step-ahead forecast. This, at first glance, sounds disconcerting. Should we not expect to do better than the naïve forecast? However, a MASE > 1 could easily come about using quite sophisticated and competitive forecasting algorithms (e.g., Athanasopoulos et al. 2011 who found MASE = 1.38 for monthly, 1.43 for quarterly, and 2.28 for yearly data). For instance, you need to keep in mind that MAE in the MASE numerator is calculated from *multistep-ahead* forecasts, whereas MAE′ in the denominator is calculated from *one-step-ahead* forecasts. It certainly is not surprising that multistep-ahead forecasts are worse than one-step-ahead (naïve) forecasts, or MAE > MAE′, or MASE > 1.

What are the advantages of MASE compared to, say, MAPE? First, it is scaled, so the MASE of forecasts for time series on different scales is comparable. Insofar, it is similar to MAPE. However, MASE has two key advantages over MAPE. First, it is defined even when one actual is

---

[1]Hyndman and Koehler (2006) give a technical reason for proposing the *in-sample* MAE as the denominator.

zero. Second, it penalizes over- and underforecasts equally, avoiding the problem we encountered in the dice-rolling example. On the other hand, MASE does have the disadvantage of being harder to interpret. A percentage error (as for MAPE) is simply easier to understand than a scaled error as a multiple of some in-sample forecast (as for MASE).

11.3   Assessing Prediction Intervals

Recall from Section 3.2 that a prediction interval of coverage q consists of a lower and an upper bound $\hat{y}^l < \hat{y}^u$ on future demand realizations y, such that we expect a certain given percentage q of future realizations to fall within the bracket $\hat{y}^l \leq y \leq \hat{y}^u$. How do we assess whether such an interval forecast is any good?

A single-interval forecast and a corresponding single-demand realization usually does not yield a lot of information. Suppose $q = 80$ percent. Even if the prediction interval captures the corresponding interval of the underlying probability distribution perfectly (which is referred to as "perfectly calibrated"), then the prediction interval is expected not to contain the true realization in one out of every five cases. If we observe just a few instances, there is little we can learn about the accuracy of our method of creating prediction intervals. Such a calibration assessment requires larger amounts of data.

Furthermore, the successful assessment of prediction intervals requires that the method of creating these intervals is fixed over time. Suppose we want to examine whether the prediction intervals provided by a forecaster are really 80 percent; if the method of how these intervals are created is not fixed during the time of observation, the forecaster could simply set very wide intervals for four of these time periods and a very narrow interval for the remaining time period, creating an 80 percent "hit rate."

In summary, in order to assess the calibration of prediction interval forecasts, we will need multiple demand observations from a time period where the method used to create these intervals was fixed. Suppose we have n interval forecasts and that k of them contain the corresponding demand realization. We can then compute the true coverage rate k/n and compare it to the so-called nominal coverage rate q. If $k/n \approx q$, then our interval forecast looks good. However, we will usually not exactly have

$k/n = q$. Thus, the question arises how large the difference between k/n and q needs to be for us to reasonably conclude that our method of constructing interval forecasts is good or bad. To this purpose, we can use a statistical concept called "Pearson's χ^2 test." We create a so-called contingency table (see Table 11.1) by noting how often our interval forecasts in fact covered the realization and how often we would have expected them to do so.

We next calculate the following *test statistic*:

$$\chi^2 = \frac{\left(k - qn\right)^2}{qn} + \frac{\left(n - k - (1 - q)n\right)^2}{(1 - q)n} \tag{46}$$

The symbol "χ" represents the small Greek letter "chi," and this test is therefore often called a "chi-squared" test. We can then examine whether this calculated value is larger than the critical value of a χ^2 distribution with 1 degree of freedom for a given α (i.e., statistical significance) level. This critical value is available in standard statistical tables or in standard statistical software, for example, using the = CHISQ.INV function in Microsoft Excel. If our calculated value from equation (46) is indeed larger than the critical value, then this can be seen as evidence for poor calibration, and we should consider improving our method of calculating prediction intervals.

As an example, let us assume we have $n = 100$ interval forecasts aiming at a nominal coverage probability of $q = 95$ percent, so we would expect $qn = 95$ of true realizations to be covered by the corresponding interval forecasts. Let us further assume that we actually observe $k = 90$ realizations that were covered by the interval forecast. Is this difference between observing $k = 90$ and expecting $qn = 95$ covered realizations statistically significant at a standard alpha level of $\alpha = 0.05$? We calculate a test statistic of $\chi^2 = (90 - 95)^2/95 + (10 - 5)^2/5 = 0.26 + 5.00 = 5.26$. The critical value of a χ^2 distribution with 1 degree of freedom for $\alpha = 0.05$, calculated for example using Microsoft Excel by "= CHISQ.INV(0.95;1)," is 3.84, which is smaller than our test statistic. We conclude that our actual

Table 11.1 Expected and observed coverage

	Covered	Not covered
Observed	k	$n - k$
Expected	qn	$(1 - q)n$

coverage is statistically significantly smaller than the nominal coverage we had aimed for and thus consider modifying our way of calculating prediction intervals.

11.4   Quality Measures for Count Data forecasts

Count data unfortunately pose particular challenges for forecast quality assessments. Some of the quality measures investigated so far can be seriously misleading for count data. For instance, the MAE does not work as expected for count data. This is a rather new discovery in the forecasting community (Morlidge 2015; Kolassa 2016a). The underlying reason is well known in statistics, but you will still find researchers and practitioners incorrectly measuring the quality of intermittent demand forecasts using MAE. After reading further, you will understand why such an approach is incorrect.

What is the problem with MAE and count data? There are two key insights to this. One is that we want a point forecast quality measure to guide us toward unbiased point forecasts. Put differently, we want any error measure to have a minimal expected value (or one of zero) if we feed it unbiased forecasts. Unfortunately, MAE does not conform to this requirement. Whereas MSE is in fact minimized and ME is zero in expectation for an unbiased forecast, MAE is not minimized by an unbiased forecast for count data. Specifically, it is easy to show that for any distribution, the forecast that minimizes the expected (mean) absolute error is not the expected value of distribution but its median (Hanley et al. 2001). This fact does not make a difference for a symmetric predictive distribution like normal distribution, since mean and median of a symmetric distribution are identical. However, the distributions we use for count data are hardly ever symmetric, and this deficiency of MAE thus becomes troubling.

Figure 11.3 shows three Poisson-distributed demand series with different means (0.05, 0.3, and 0.6), along with probability mass histograms turned sideways. Importantly, in all three cases, the median of the Poisson distribution is zero, meaning that the point forecast that minimizes MAE is zero. Turning this argument around, suppose we use MAE to find the "best" forecasting algorithm for a number of count data series. We find that a flat zero-point forecast minimizes MAE. This is not surprising after

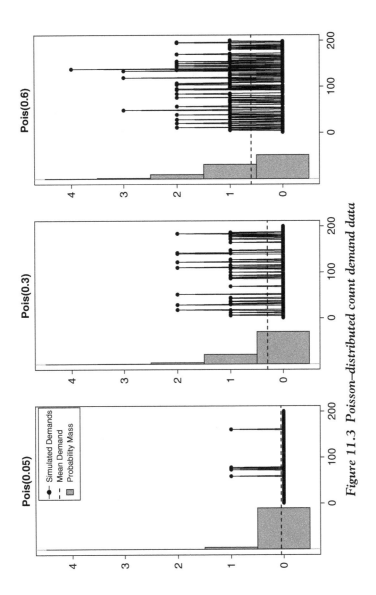

Figure 11.3 Poisson–distributed count demand data

the discussion above. However, a flat zero forecast is obviously not useful. The inescapable conclusion is that *we need to be very careful about using MAE for assessing point forecasts for count data!*

Unfortunately, this realization implies that all point forecast quality measures that are only scaled multiples of MAE are equally useless for count data. Specifically, this applies to MASE and wMAPE, which in addition is undefined if *all* demands in the evaluation period are zero. Finally, almost needless to say, MAPE does not make any sense for intermittent data, since APEs are undefined if $y = 0$. Happily, some quality measures do work (mostly) "as advertised" for count data. The ME is still a valid measure of bias. However, of course, highly intermittent demands can, simply by chance, have long strings of consecutive zero demands, so any nonzero forecast may look biased. Thus, detecting bias is even harder for count data than for continuous data.

Similarly, the MSE still retains its property of being minimized by the expectation of future realizations. Therefore, we can still use MSE to guide us toward unbiased forecasts. As discussed above, MSE can still not be meaningfully compared between time series of different levels. One could, however, scale RMSE by the series' overall mean to obtain a scaled error measure that is comparable between series.

11.5   Key Takeaways

- There are numerous forecast accuracy measures.
- Different accuracy measures measure different things. There is no one "best" accuracy KPI. Consider looking at multiple ones.
- If you have only a single time series or series on similar scales, use MSE or MAE.
- If you have multiple series at different scales, use scaled or percentage errors. However, remember that these percentage errors can introduce asymmetries with respect to how they penalize over- and underforecasting.
- Always look at bias. Be aware that MAE and MAPE can mislead you into biased forecasts.

CHAPTER 12

Forecasting Competitions

So far, we considered many different forecasting methods, from purely statistical ones to judgmental ones. And, of course, we have only scratched the surface in this book; there are many more established forecasting methods. In addition, if you want to implement a forecasting system, each software vendor will have his/her own variants on these basic methods, as well as home-grown, possibly proprietary algorithms. How do we decide which of these forecasting methods are the best for our data?

To decide between many different forecasting methods, we can run a so-called *forecasting competition*, in which different methods compete to provide the best forecast. Such forecasting competitions are not entirely straightforward to run. We therefore devote an entire chapter to describing the generally accepted best way of running them.

12.1 Planning

Similar to a randomized controlled trial in the field of medicine, a forecasting competition needs to be specified and planned in advance. Changing parameters in mid-competition may be problematic. Including additional data after the first data delivery will likely lead to a larger data-cleansing effort than if all the data had been provided at once. Changing accuracy measures may mean that models change dramatically, possibly invalidating earlier work.

Think about the decision your forecast is supporting. Do you want it for planning marketing and promotions? Or for short-range ordering and replenishment decisions? This will have an impact on the data you will need, in particular in terms of granularity along the product, time, and location dimensions (see Chapter 14), as well as on the forecast horizon and on what forecast accuracy measures (see Chapter 11) make sense. You may need forecasts for different processes, in which case you may need to think about how you want to deal with aggregation and forecast hierarchies (again, see Chapter 14).

Plan for an iterated process. If the people that actually perform the forecasting are already intimately familiar with your data—for instance, because they belong to an established forecasting group within your business and have indeed been forecasting your time series for years—they may already have a very good understanding of your data, its idiosyncrasies, and your processes. However, if you perform the forecasting competition on data from a new subsidiary, or if you involve external consultants or third-party forecasting software vendors, they will need to understand your data before they can calculate meaningful forecasts. This is best done via live discussions, either face-to-face or at least via web conferencing. Written data descriptions are always useful, but forecasting experts will always have additional questions. After all, you would not expect your doctor to provide a reliable diagnosis based on a written description of your symptoms alone either!

As discussed in Chapter 11, there are numerous forecast accuracy measures. Invest some time in choosing good ones to use for comparison. Certain measures may be unusable for your data, like MAPE for data with zeros, or may lead to biased forecasts, like MAE for low-volume data. If you use multiple series on different scales, make sure your accuracy measures can meaningfully be compared and summarized across scales, by using percentage or scaled error measures. Do think about using more than one error measure—each performance index is better than others at detecting different problems in your forecasts. In any case, you should always assess forecasts on both bias and accuracy, as described in Chapter 11.

If your forecasting competition involves external parties, do not be afraid of involving them already in an early planning stage. After all, you are planning on trusting these people's software and expertise with a mission-critical process in your business, so you should be able to trust that they know what they are doing. A dedicated forecasting software provider or forecasting consultant may well know more about forecasting and have more expertise with more different data sets than your in-house forecasting group, although your in-house experts will likely know your data better. Tap this external expertise. Discuss your business and your data with the vendor. Consider their suggestions about what kind of data to include in the forecasting competition. Of course, the vendor will be looking out for himself first, but that does not mean his/her proposals will be useless. In addition, this kind of early discussion allows you to gauge his expertise and his commitment. Try to get subject matter experts to participate in these discussions, not just salespeople.

12.2   Data

After you have thought about what you need the forecast for, you can start collecting data. Make the data set representative. If the forecast competition aims at identifying a method to forecast a small number of highly aggregated time series, perform the competition on a small number of highly aggregated time series. If you are looking for an automated method that can perform well on thousands of series, use a large data set with thousands of series. If you only give out 20 series, the forecasters will tune each model by hand, but that will not be possible in a production environment with thousands of series—so use more data to begin with.

Does your day-to-day data contain outliers or invalid periods? Make sure to include such series. Conversely, do you plan on forecasting only precleaned data? Then preclean the data in the same way. Do you have causal drivers, like promotions or weather? Then include these effects in the data set you provide. As in our example in Chapter 8, the causal effects may or may not improve the forecast, but you will not know if you do not try. Try to make the data set you use for the competition as representative as possible for the actual forecasting task you need for your business.

However, remember that, as noted in Chapter 8, causal models require *forecasts* of causal drivers. If your business depends heavily on weather, your demand forecast will need to rely on weather *forecasts*. If you run your forecasting competition using *actual* weather instead of the forecasted weather, you are pretending that you know the future weather perfectly, and your forecasts will be better than if you relied on weather forecasts instead. Your causal models will appear to perform better than they really will in a production environment. Thus, make sure to include *forecasts* of your causal drivers for the forecasting period. As a rule of thumb, a forecast prepared in a particular time period should only use the information available in that time period.

12.3   Procedure

In principle, the procedure of a forecasting competition is simple: collect data, calculate forecasts, and evaluate the forecasts. The data selection and collection has been discussed in previous chapters, so let us focus on the other steps here.

One key aspect in forecasting competitions is to hold back evaluation data. For instance, you could collect demand data from 3 years, give out the demands of the first 2 years, keeping the third year's demands for evaluation, and require forecasts for this third year. If the forecaster knows the third year's demands, he/she may very well succumb to the temptation to "snoop," tweaking his/her forecasts until they perform best on the *known* evaluation sample—but of course that will not work in an actual production environment. Avoid the temptation to cheat, especially for external vendors.

This discussion leads us to a related aspect: why should we use separate evaluation data? Is not it enough to assess how well a forecasting method fits the historical data? If one method performs better in-sample than another method, should it not yield better forecasts, too? Unfortunately, this appealing logic does not work. As a rule of thumb, more complex models (e.g., a seasonal vs. a nonseasonal model, or a trend model vs. a non-trend model) will always yield better in-sample fits than simpler models. But beyond some optimal complexity, in-sample fit keeps on improving, while out-of-sample forecast accuracy starts deteriorating. The reason is that the more complex models start fitting to noise instead of capturing a signal. Figure 12.1 illustrates this, using the "hard to forecast" series from Figure 1.1 and giving MSEs in thousands. We fit four different models of increasing complexity to the first 12 months of data and forecast the last 6 months. As we see, the more complex the models are, as reflected in more and more flexible influences of time, the closer the in-sample fit mirrors historical data and the lower in-sample MSE becomes—but out-of-sample forecasts get worse and worse. Thus, in-sample fit is not

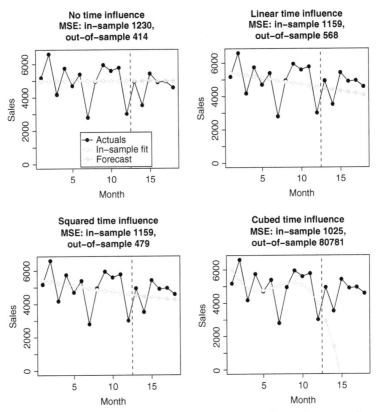

Figure 12.1 In-Sample and Out of Out-of-Sample performance for more complex models

a reliable guide to out-of-sample forecast accuracy, and we should never rely on in-sample accuracy to judge a forecasting method.

Let us continue with the actual procedure of a forecasting competition. You can run either "single origin" or "rolling origin" forecasts. In a single-origin setting as in Figure 12.1, you might give out 12 months of data and require forecasts for the next 6 months, allowing you to assess forecasts on horizons between 1 and 6 months ahead. In a rolling-origin forecast competition, you would give out 12 months of data, require 6 months of forecasts. . . then give out the actual demand for one more month, this time requiring 5 months of forecasts . . . then give out an additional month's demands . . . you get the idea. In such a rolling origin set-up, the forecast method can learn from each additional month of historical data and adapt. This more closely mimics real forecasting processes, which would also be repeated and iterated, adapting to new information. Plus, it gives you more forecasts to base your evaluation on. On the other hand, you need to organize *multiple* exchanges of forecast and actual data and keep careful track of a forecast's "vintage": Was a given forecast for June a one-step-ahead forecast based on data until May or a two-step-ahead forecast based on data through April? Overall, rolling-origin forecast competitions are more realistic, but require more effort, especially if you communicate with one or multiple external vendors—if your internal forecasting group runs the competition, rolling origins may simply require a few more lines of code.

Finally, in evaluating the forecasts of different methods, look at matters from different angles. Summarize forecasts per series (if you have more than one forecast per series), then summarize these summaries over all series—for instance, taking averages of errors. If you consider different forecasting horizons, look at how errors behave for one-step, two-step, and longer-range forecasts. Did you include series with outliers (in the historical or the future period) in your data set? Or series with strong seasonality or driven especially strongly by certain causal factors? If so, check how your forecasts performed on those. Do not only look at averages of errors over series, but also at forecasts that performed extremely badly. Two methods may yield similar errors on average, but one of the two methods may break down badly in certain circumstances. Such rare spectacular failures can badly erode users' trust in a forecasting system, even if forecasts are good on average, so you should include forecasting methods' robustness in your overall assessment. Finally, consider discussing results with the forecasters, whether internal or external—you may learn interesting things this way.

12.4   Additional Aspects

Of course, the main focus of our forecasting competition lies on forecasting and accuracy. However, as discussed above, forecasting does not happen in a vacuum. We want forecasts in the first place to support business decisions, like how many units of a product to produce. It is likely not the forecast itself but the final business decision (how much to produce) that impacts the bottom line. Good forecasts do not earn or save money—good inventories do. And depending on subsequent decision-making processes, forecasts with very different accuracies may yield very similar impacts on the bottom line. For instance, if true demand is 600 and two methods yield forecasts of 700 and 900 units, respectively, then the first method is obviously more accurate. However, if your operations constrain you to produce in batches of 1,000, both forecasts would have led to the same business decision—to produce 1,000 units—the same service level and the same overstock; so for all practical purposes, spending additional funds to use the more accurate forecast would have been a waste. (However, if such situations occur frequently, you may want to try to make your production more flexible.) Thus, it makes sense to simulate the entire process, including both forecasting and subsequent decision making.

Finally, there are other aspects of a forecasting method to consider beyond forecasting accuracy. A method may be extremely accurate but require a lot of manual tuning by statistical experts, which can become expensive. Further, more complex forecasting methods can be more difficult to sell to other managers, and the forecasts resulting from these methods stand a higher chance of being ignored even if they are more accurate (Taylor and Thomas 1982). Or the method may simply take too much time to run—one technology may give you all your operational forecasts within seconds, while the other may need to run overnight. Faster forecasting allows more scenario planning, like changing causal variables and simulating the impact on demands. One forecasting software suite may be standalone and require expensive integration into your ERP system, while another one may already be integrated or may have well-defined interfaces that connect well with your existing databases.

12.5 Key Takeaways

- Plan out your forecasting competition ahead of time.
- Make sure your competition mirrors your real forecasting situation in terms of data and knowledge and in the decisions that must be supported by the forecast.
- Do not be afraid of involving external experts in setting up a forecasting competition. Of course, make sure not to be taken for a ride.

- *Always* hold back the evaluation data.
- Evaluate forecasts by slicing your data in different ways, to get an overall understanding of a forecasting method's strengths and weaknesses.
- Forecast accuracy is not everything. Look at the larger picture, from decisions made based on the forecast to ease of integration of a forecasting software.

PART V

Forecasting Organization

CHAPTER 13

Sales and Operations Planning

13.1 Forecasting Organization

Much of this book has treated forecasting as a predominantly statistical exercise—making use of information within the organization to reduce demand uncertainty. In practice, forecasting is as much an organizational exercise as a statistical one: Information is diffused throughout the organization, and the forecast has many stakeholders all of whom require the forecast as an input to their planning processes. Understanding demand forecasting requires an understanding of not only the statistical methods used to produce a forecast but also the process of how an organization creates a forecast and uses it for decision making.

Managing this process well is the realm of Sales and Operations Planning (S&OP). Given that S&OP has been around for a while, best practices for such processes are now established (e.g., Lapide 2014). There is an input and an output side to this process. On the input side, a good S&OP process supports sharing relevant information about the demand forecast. The emphasis here is on marketing and sales to share upcoming product launches, acquisition of new customers, planned promotions, and similar information with those responsible for forecasting to help them in the process. At the same time, other functions such as operations need to share relevant input data into the planning process as well, such as the inventory position, capacity available, and so forth. On the output side are a set of coordinated plans that all use the same information as input. Marketing develops a plan for promotions and demand management. Operations develop production and procurement plans. Finance develops cash flow plans and uses numbers, in coordination with the other departments, to communicate with investors. Human resources develop a personnel plan based on the same forecast data. If this process goes well, the organization will be coordinated, and decisions and plans will be based on all available information. If this process does not go well, information will be hoarded, forecasts will be influenced by individual members, and different functions of the organization lack coordination. The result will be highly inaccurate forecasts and, as a consequence, promotions that may not be backed by capacity and forecasts shared with investors that bear little resemblance to actual plans of the organization, thus damaging the firm's credibility.

An S&OP process is a monthly process within an organization to enhance information sharing and coordinate plans across the organization. It usually involves a cross-functional team from marketing, operations, finance, and sometimes human resources. There are typically five different steps in an S&OP process. Beginning with *data gathering*, representatives from different functions share relevant information with each other and develop a common set of business assumptions that go into the forecast. In the actual *demand planning* stage, the team finalizes promotion and pricing decisions and agrees on a consensus forecast. This forecast is then used to develop sales targets for the sales function. Afterwards in the *supply planning* stage, inventory, production, capacity, and procurement decisions are made according to the forecast. Further, if shortages are expected, rationing and prioritization policies are developed; if major risk events are considered, contingencies are developed and shared with all members of the team. Finally, in the *pre-executive meeting*, senior management can adjust any outcomes of the S&OP process. The finance function, in particular, sometimes has a veto power at this step, to enable better cash flow planning and investor communications. Finally, all relevant plans are discussed and finalized with top management during the *executive meeting*.

13.2   Organizational Barriers

There are two essential barriers to overcome in order to make this process work: incentives and organizational boundaries. The former barrier stems from the fact that incentives across different functions are not aligned, and often no one is held accountable for the quality of forecasts. Managers in marketing or sales may have an incentive to lowball the forecast, since they understand that their sales targets are often set depending on the forecast, and thus lowering the forecast is an easy way to make their targets more obtainable. Or they may have an incentive to inflate the forecast, since they understand that this will push operations to make more products available, thus decreasing the chances of a stockout happening and thereby increasing sales-related bonuses. Managers in operations, on the contrary, are often compensated based on costs; one way to keep less inventory is to lowball the forecast and thereby lower production volumes. Finance will chip in here as well, since they will use the forecast to manage investor expectations. These incentives will inevitably lead to a confusion of forecasting and decision making; the actual forecast thereby becomes not one number to coordinate all activities but a playball of organizational politics.

The latter barrier is a result of different functional backgrounds and social identities. On a very basic level, people in marketing may have studied different topics than people in operations; they may have had a different entry route into the organization as well. As a result, their way of perceiving and communicating about organizational realities may be very different, leading to challenges in managing a cross-functional team involving both groups. The units they forecast may also be different—whereas finance forecasts revenue in US dollars, marketing may predict market shares and operations is interested in units of production. While these units can usually be easily converted, they represent a natural barrier to overcome, and the conversion of these units should be standardized upfront. Last but not least, having different functions always implies different social identities that are difficult to overcome. Representatives from marketing will feel a natural allegiance to their function, as will representatives from operations. While such identification usually creates more trust within the group, it creates distrust between groups. Successfully managing a cross-functional S&OP team thus requires not only establishing standardized norms of communication, it also requires breaking down functional barriers to build trust between representatives of different functions.

One approach to solve these barriers is to create a forecasting group that is organizationally separate from all other participating functions;

this promotes accountability for forecast accuracy. It also creates professionalism and allows people associated with this group to be compensated on forecasting performance. A survey on forecasting practice found that 38 percent of responding organizations have introduced a separate functional area for forecasting, and 62 percent of those separate functional areas owned the forecasting process (McCarthy et al. 2006). An essential advantage is that forecasters in this area can be compensated based on the accuracy of forecasts without creating asymmetry in their incentive systems; incentivizing forecasting in all other areas requires very careful calibration to offset the existing incentives in these areas to over- or underforecast (Scheele, Slikker, and Thonemann 2014). If creating a separate function is organizationally impossible, then the people participating in S&OP planning should de-emphasize their functional association. For example, it may be possible to completely take the participating employees out of their functional incentive systems and reward them according to firm performance or according to forecasting performance instead.

Another essential aspect is to demystify the forecasts; all those involved in the forecasting process should be familiar with the data, software, and algorithms used in creating forecasts. Assumptions made should be documented and transparent to everyone involved, and individuals should be held accountable for their judgment. As we emphasize in Chapter 11, it is ex post always possible to tell whether adjustments made to a statistical forecast were actually helpful or harmful to forecasting performance if one takes a longer term perspective. As such, an interesting avenue to resolve incentive issues in S&OP may be to use past forecast accuracy coming from different functions to determine the future weight that is given to these different functional forecasts when calculating a consensus forecast. Functions that bias their forecast will thus quickly lose their ability to influence the consensus forecast, creating an incentive for them to avoid unnecessarily biasing the forecast.

A good case study of transforming an S&OP process is given by Oliva and Watson (2009). The authors study an electronics manufacturer that started off with a dysfunctional forecasting process; the company had three different functions (sales, operations, and finance) creating three different forecasts; the only information sharing happened in nonstandardized spreadsheet and hallway conversations. The company proceeded to generate a process that started by (1) creating a separate group that was responsible for the statistical side of forecasting, (2) creating a common assumptions package where each function would contribute their key information about the development of the business, (3) allowing the different functions to generate separate forecasts based on the same information but then (4) integrating these forecasts using a weighted average, where the weight attributed to each function depended on past accuracy, and (5) limiting revisions to this initial consensus forecast to only those instances where real data could be brought up to support any modifications to the forecast. The result was a stark increase in forecasting performance. Whereas company forecasts had an accuracy (1-MAPE) of only 50 percent before this redesign, this accuracy jumped up to almost 90 percent after restructuring the S&OP process.

13.3   Key Takeaways

- Forecasting is as much a social and an organizational activity as a statistical one.
- Employees' functional background may incentivize them to influence the forecast in ways that are not optimal for the business as a whole. Consider changing their incentives to align with getting an unbiased forecast.
- It may be very beneficial to organizationally separate forecasting out from traditional functional areas.
- Similarly, employees' background may influence the way they think and communicate about forecasts. Keep this in mind and work for open communication.

CHAPTER 14

Forecasting Hierarchies

14.1 Multivariate Time Series

So far, this book has focused on forecasting individual demand time series, one at a time. Limiting our discussion in this way was useful to create focus; however, in most practical situations, forecasters may have to deal with thousands of time series at once. Further, these time series are related to each other, either because products are substitutes or complements or because hierarchical levels overlap. Further, forecasters have an interest in many different hierarchical levels. Consider, for example, that several time series may represent a portfolio of products; products are grouped into categories, but also in turn are divided into multiple stock-keeping units (SKUs) as variants of the product, differing in color, size, flavor, and so forth. The more a market has been horizontally and vertically differentiated into different target groups, the more does forecasting a product really mean forecasting a multitude of SKUs. Aggregate production planning may simply require a volume forecast at the product level, but a detailed production and procurement planning will also require more precise forecasts related to the mix of products demanded. Promotion planning will require forecasts at the product or product category level. Similarly, the overlap in the bills of material in our product portfolio may create a hierarchical divide: Suppose we bake both blueberry and chocolate chip muffins. We need forecasts of demand for both muffin types separately to plan production, but when sourcing flour, we only need a forecast of our total flour demand and do not care which type of muffin a particular pound of flour ends up in.

Another reason for recognizing forecast hierarchies lies in the spatial separation of markets; continents or sales regions are often divided into countries, which in turn are divided into states or markets. A retail company may need, for example, store-specific forecasts for particular SKUs to determine the store replenishment policy, but will also need forecasts for the same SKUs at their distribution center to in turn plan the replenishment of the distribution center. Similarly, in business-to-business settings, salespeople may need customer-specific forecasts, whereas production planners need a forecast of the total demand across all customers. Finally, time can be seen as another form of hierarchy in forecasts. An online fashion retailer may need forecasts of daily goods movements to schedule the warehouse workforce. The same retailer will also need forecasts for the entire fashion season, which can range from a few weeks to a few months, to procure products from the countries of origin.

To add to the complexity of forecasting hierarchies, the different hierarchies are often crossed with each other. For instance, a consumer goods manufacturer may be interested in sales to retailer A in region X, but also

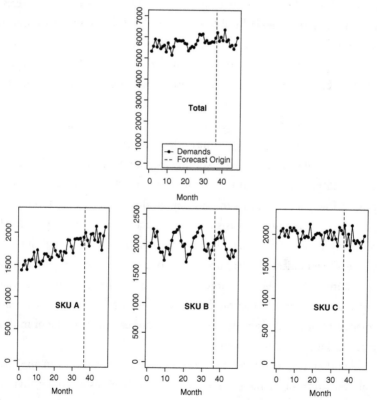

Figure 14.1 An example hierarchy with three SKUs' time series

in sales to retailer B in region Y, crossing geographical and customer hierarchies. This example also illustrates that these two hierarchies are often closely aligned, but not identical. The challenge in forecasting hierarchies lies in creating a consistent set of forecasts at different levels.

If we ignore the hierarchical and interdependent nature of our forecasting portfolio, we could take the time series at different aggregation levels—say, sales of SKU A, sales of SKU B, and total sales in the category containing A and B—as different time series and forecast them separately. The problem with this approach is that forecasts will not be hierarchically consistent. Whereas *historical* demands of different SKUs add up to total *historical* category demand, the *forecasts* of different SKUs will almost certainly *not* add up to the forecast on the category level. "The sum of the forecasts is not equal to the forecast of the sum." There are various ways of addressing this problem, all with their advantages and disadvantages, which we will describe next. Figure 14.1 shows a simple example hierarchy consisting of three SKUs, each with 3 years of history and 1 hold-out year.

14.2   Bottom-Up Forecasting

The simplest form of hierarchical forecasting is the bottom-up approach. This method works just the way it sounds: We take the time series at the most granular level, forecast each of these disaggregate series, and then aggregate the forecasts up to the desired level of aggregation (without separately forecasting at higher levels). This method is indeed often used without being identified as such, especially for bills of materials. For instance, every bakery that forecasts its sales of blueberry and chocolate chip muffins separately multiplies each forecast number with a specific number of cups of flour and finally aggregates the separate forecasts for flour to get a final aggregate flour demand forecast. This corresponds to bottom-up forecasting with conversion factors (the number of cups of flour per dozen muffins).

One advantage of this approach lies in its simplicity. It is very easy to implement this method, and the process of bottom-up forecasting offers only little opportunity for mistakes. In addition, it is also very easy to explain this approach to a nontechnical audience. The method is also very robust: even if we badly misforecast one series, the effect will be

largely confined to this series and the level of aggregation just above it—
the grand total will not be perturbed a lot. In addition, bottom-up forecasting works very well with causal forecasts, since you *know* the value of
your causal effect, like the price, on the most fine-grained level. Finally,
bottom-up forecasting can lead to less errors in judgment for nonsubsti-
tutable products, increasing the accuracy of forecasts if human judgment
plays an essential role in the forecasting process (Kremer, Siemsen, and
Thomas 2016).

However, bottom-up forecasting also offers challenges. First, the
more granular and disaggregated the historical time series are, the more
intermittent they will be, especially if different hierarchies are crossed.
On a single SKU × store × day level, many demand histories may con-
sist of little else but zeros. On a higher aggregation level, for example, SKU × week across all stores, the time series may be more regular.

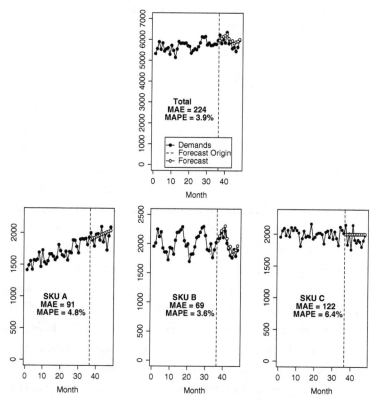

Figure 14.2 Bottom-up forecasts

Forecasts for intermittent demands are notoriously hard, unreliable, and noisy (see Chapter 9). Second, while *specific* causal factors will be well defined on a fine-grained level, *general* dynamics will be very hard to detect. For instance, a set of time series may be seasonal, but the seasonal signal may be very weak and difficult to detect and exploit on the level of single series. Seasonality may be visible on an aggregate level but not at the granular level. In such a case, fitting seasonality on the lower level may even decrease accuracy (Kolassa 2016b).

Figure 14.2 shows bottom-up forecasting applied to the example hierarchy from Figure 14.1. The trend in SKU A and seasonality in SKU B are captured well, and the forecast on the total level consequently shows *both* weak trend and weak seasonality.

14.3 Top-Down Forecasting

Top-down forecasting is a somewhat more complex method than bottom-up forecasting. As the name implies, this process means that we first forecast at the highest level of hierarchy (or hierarchies) and then disaggregate forecasts down to lower levels as required. What is more complex about top-down forecasting? The added complexity comes from the fact that we need to decide on how exactly to *disaggregate* the higher level forecasts. And this in turn is nothing else than forecasting the proportions in which, say, different SKUs will make up total category sales in a given future month. Of course, these proportions could change over time.

One way of forecasting proportions is to disregard the changes in proportions over time. Following this approach, we could disaggregate by calculating proportions of all historical sales, then use these to disaggregate future total forecasts ("disaggregation by historical proportions"). This method implies betting that historical proportions will continue to be valid in the future. Similarly, we could use only the most recent proportions to disaggregate our predictions ("disaggregation by recent proportions"). This would imply betting on proportions that constantly change, and the debate from Section 5.3 on stability vs. change is as valid in this context as it was before. Alternatively, we could forecast the totals as above, but also forecast lower level demand series and break down total forecasts proportionally to lower level forecasts ("disaggregation by forecast proportions").

Any number of forecast algorithms—seasonal or not, trended or not—could be used for this purpose. The forecasts for the top level (used to forecast total demands) do not need to be calculated using the same method as the forecasts for lower levels (only used to derive breakdown proportions).

On the plus side, top-down forecasting is still very simple to use and explain, almost as simple as bottom-up forecasting. And in explaining a concrete implementation of the process, the question of how to forecast the disaggregation proportions (which is a more complex issue) can often be relegated to a technical footnote. Further, top-down forecasting can have the advantage of better incorporating inter-relationships between time series, particularly in the context of substitutable products (Kremer, Siemsen, and Thomas 2016). On the down side, the other advantages and disadvantages of top-down forecasting mirror those of the bottom-up approach. Whereas bottom-up forecasting is very robust to

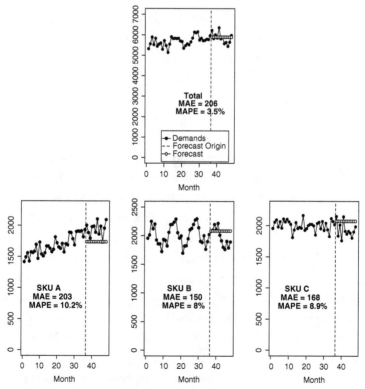

Figure 14.3 Top-down forecasts

single misforecasts, top-down forecasting faithfully pushes every error on the top level down to every other level. Furthermore, top-down forecasting often gets the *total* forecast right, but the way how this total is composed of separate lower level demands crucially depends on how we forecast the future proportions—if demand gradually shifts from SKU A to B because of slow changes in customer taste, we need to include this explicitly in our proportion forecasts, or we will not see this market shift in the disaggregated forecasts.

While causal factors like prices are well defined for bottom-up forecasting (although their effect may be hard to detect; see Kolassa 2016b), they are not as well defined for top-down forecasting. Prices are defined on single SKUs, not on "all products" level. We could of course use averages of causal factors, for example, average prices in product hierarchies. However, if we use unweighted averages, we relatively overweight slow-selling products—and if we use weighted averages of prices, weighting each SKU's price with its sales to account for its importance in the product hierarchy, then we have to solve the problem of how to calculate these weights for the *forecast* period. We might be tempted to calculate a weighted average price, where we weight each SKU's price with its forecast sales, but this would be putting the cart before the horse, since forecasting the bottom levels is exactly what we are trying to do.

Figure 14.3 shows top-down forecasting, using disaggregation by historical proportions, applied to the example hierarchy from Figure 14.1. As trend and seasonal signal are only weak on the total level, the automatic model selection picks single exponential smoothing. Consequently, the disaggregated forecasts on SKU level do not exhibit trend or seasonality, either. Top-down forecasting is obviously not appropriate in this example, because the bottom-level time series exhibit obvious but different signals (trend in SKU A, seasonality in SKU B, nothing in SKU C). If the bottom-level series exhibit similar but weak signals, top-down forecasting may perform better than bottom-up (Kolassa 2016b).

14.4 Middle-Out Forecasting

Middle-out forecasting is a middle road between bottom-up and top-down forecasting. Pick a "middle" level in your hierarchy. Aggregate historical data up to this level. Forecast. Disaggregate the forecasts back down and aggregate them up as required. This approach combines the advantages and disadvantages of bottom-up and top-down forecasting. Demands aggregated to a middle level in the hierarchy will be less sparse than on the bottom level, so we will get much better defined seasonal and similar signals. Similarly, it may be easier to derive aggregate causal factors when going to a middle level than when going all the way to the top level. For instance, if all products of a given brand have a "20 percent off" promotion, we can aggregate historical demands to total brand sales and apply a common "20 percent off promotion" predictor to the aggregate. (However we would need to explicitly model *differential* sensitivity to price reductions for different SKUs in the brand—a simple approach would yield the same forecast uplift for all products.)

Once we have the forecasts on a middle level, aggregating them up is just as simple as aggregating up bottom-level forecasts in a bottom-up approach. And conversely, disaggregating middle-level forecasts down to a more fine-grained level is similar to disaggregating top-level forecasts in a top-down approach: we again need to decide on how to forecast disaggregation proportions, for instance (the simplest way), doing disaggregation by historical proportions.

14.5   Optimal Reconciliation Forecasting

One recently developed approach, and a completely new way of looking at hierarchical forecasting, is the so-called optimal reconciliation approach (Hyndman et al. 2011; Hyndman and Athanasopoulos 2014). The key insight underlying this approach is to go back to the original problem of hierarchical forecasting: if we separately forecast all of our time series on all aggregation levels, then the point forecasts will not be sum consistent. They will not "fit" together. If things do not "fit" the way they are, we can calculate a "best (possible) fit" between forecasts made directly for a particular hierarchical level and forecasts made indirectly by either summing up or disaggregating from different levels, using methods similar to regression. We will not go into the statistical details of this method—readers can refer to Hyndman et al. (2011) for these or look at the "hts" package for R.

Calculating optimally reconciled hierarchical forecasts provides a number of advantages. One benefit is that the final forecasts use *all* component forecasts on *all* aggregation levels. We can use different forecasting methods on different levels or even mix statistical and judgmental forecasts. Thus, we can model dynamics on the levels where they are best fit, for example, price influences on a brand level and seasonality on a category level. We therefore do not need to worry about making hard decisions about how to aggregate causal factors—if it is unclear how to aggregate a factor, we can simply leave it out in forecasting on this particular aggregation level. And it turns out that the optimal reconciliation approach frequently yields better forecasts on *all* aggregation levels, beating bottom-up, top-down, and middle-out in accuracy, because it combines so many different sources of information.

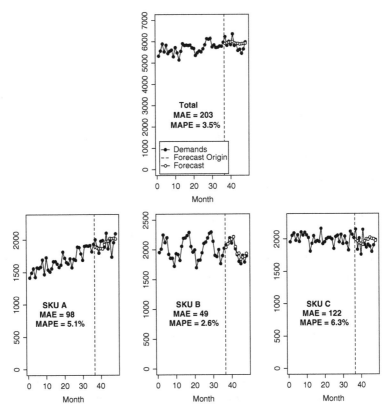

Figure 14.4 Optimal combination forecasts

Optimal reconciliation of course also has drawbacks. One is that the specifics are somewhat harder to understand and to communicate than for the three "classical" approaches. Another disadvantage is that while it works very well with "small" hierarchies, it quickly poses computational and numerical challenges for realistic hierarchies in demand forecasting, which could contain thousands of nodes arranged in multiple levels in multiple crossed hierarchies. For single (noncrossed) hierarchies, or for crossed hierarchies that are all of height 2 ("grouped" hierarchies), one can do smart algorithmic tricks (Hyndman, Lee, and Wang 2016), but the general case of crossed hierarchies is still intractable.

Figure 14.4 shows optimal combination forecasting applied to the example hierarchy from Figure 14.1. As in bottom-up forecasting (Figure 14.2), the trend in SKU A and seasonality in SKU B are captured well, and the forecast on the total level consequently shows *both* weak trend and weak seasonality. However, note that errors for optimal combination forecasts are even lower than for bottom-up forecasts. This is a frequent finding.

14.6   Other Approaches

Hierarchical structures allow forecast improvements even if we are not really interested in hierarchical *forecasts* per se. For example, we may only need SKU-level forecasts but still be interested in whether product groups allow us to improve these SKU-level forecasts. For instance, seasonality is often more easily estimated on aggregate levels. We could therefore aggregate data to higher levels, then extract seasonal patterns or indices, deseasonalize lower-level time series, forecast the deseasonalized series, and finally apply the group-level seasonal indices again to properly incorporate seasonality at the lower level. Mohammadipour et al. (2015) explain this approach in more depth. The same method could be applied in calculating the effects of trend, promotions, or any other dynamic on an aggregate level, even if we are not interested in forecasts on this aggregate level as such.

One point should be kept in mind when we forecast hierarchical data: the hierarchies we are given are often not set up with forecasting in mind. For instance, products grouped by supplier may sort different varieties of apples into different hierarchies, although they appear the same to customers and would profit from hierarchical forecasting. It may be worthwhile to create separate "forecasting hierarchies" and to check whether these improve forecasts (Mohammadipour et al. 2015).

14.7   Key Takeaways

- If you have a small hierarchy and can use dedicated software like R's hts package or have people sufficiently versed in linear algebra who can code the reconciliation themselves, go for the optimal reconciliation approach. If the optimal reconciliation approach is not possible, use one of the other (i.e., bottom-up, top-down, or middle-out) methods.

- If you are most interested in top-level forecasts, with the other levels "nice to have," or if you are worried about extensive substitutability among your products, use top-down forecasting.

- If you are most interested in bottom-level forecasts, with the other levels "nice to have," or many of your products are not substitutes, use bottom-up forecasting.

- If you cannot decide, use middle-out forecasting. Either pick a middle level that makes sense from a business point of view, for example, the level in the product hierarchy at which you plan marketing activities, or try different levels and look which one yields the best forecast overall.

- Never be afraid of including hierarchical information, even if you are not interested in forecasts at higher levels of aggregation. It may improve your lower-level forecasts.

- Consider creating additional "forecasting hierarchies" if that helps getting the job done.

References

Abraham, Bovas, and Johannes Ledolter. 1983. *Statistical Methods for Forecasting*. New York, NY: John Wiley & Sons, Inc.

Ali, Mohammad M, John E Boylan, and Aris A Syntetos. 2015. "Forecast Errors and Inventory Performance under Forecast Information Sharing." *International Journal of Forecasting* 28 (4): 830–41.

Anderson, Eric T, Gavan J Fitzsimons, and Duncan Simester. 2006. "Measuring and Mitigating the Costs of Stockouts." *Management Science* 52 (11): 1751–63.

Angrist, Joshua D, and Joern-Steffen Pischke. 2009. *Mostly Harmless Econometrics*. Princeton, NJ: Princeton University Press.

Armstrong, J. Scott 2001. "Combining Forecasts." In *Principles of Forecasting*, edited by J Scott Armstrong, Kluwer Aca, 1–19. Norwell, MA: Kluwer.

Armstrong, J. Scott, and Fred Collopy. 1998. "Integration of Statistical Methods and Judgment for Time Series Forecasting: Principles from Empirical Research." In *Forecasting with Judgment*, edited by George Wright and Paul Goodwin, 269–93. New York, NY: John Wiley & Sons Ltd.

Athanasopoulos, George, Rob J Hyndman, Haiyan Song, and Doris C Wu. 2011. "The Tourism Forecasting Competition." *International Journal of Forecasting* 27 (3): 822–44.

Batchelor, Roy. 2010. "Worst-Case Scenarios in Forecasting: How Bad Can Things Get?" *Foresight* 18: 27–32.

Berry, Tim. 2010. *Sales and Market Forecasting for Entrepreneurs*. New York, NY: Business Expert Press.

Biais, Bruno, and Martin Weber. 2009. "Hindsight Bias, Risk Perception, and Investment Performance." *Management Science* 55 (6): 1018–29.

Boulaksil, Youssef, and Philip Hans Franses. 2009. "Experts' Stated Behavior." *Interfaces* 39 (2): 168–71.

Boylan, John E, and Aris A Syntetos. 2006. "Accuracy and Accuracy Implication Metrics for Intermittent Demand." *Foresight* 4: 39–42.

Cachon, Gérard P, and Martin A Lariviere. 1999. "An Equilibrium Analysis of Linear, Proportional and Uniform Allocation of Scarce Capacity." *IIE Transactions* 31 (9): 835–49.

Chatfield, Chris. 2001. "Prediction Intervals for Time-Series Forecasting." In *Principles of Forecasting*, edited by J Scott Armstrong, 475–94. New York, NY: Springer.

———. 2007. "Confessions of a Pragmatic Forecaster." *Foresight* 6: 3–9.

Chatfield, Chris, Anne B Koehler, J Keith Ord, and Ralph D Snyder. 2001. "A New Look at Models for Exponential Smoothing." *Journal of the Royal Statistical Society: Series D* 50 (2): 147–59.

Choi, Hyunyoung, and Hal Varian. 2012. "Predicting the Present with Google Trends." *Economic Record* 88 (Suppl.1): 2–9.

Clarke, Simon. 2006. "Managing the Introduction of a Structured Forecast Process: Transformation Lessons from Coca-Cola Enterprises Inc." *Foresight* 4: 21–25.

Clemen, Robert T. 1989. "Combining Forecasts: A Review and Annotated Bibliography." *International Journal of Forecasting* 5 (4): 559–83.

Cooper, Lee G, Penny Baron, Wayne Levy, Michael Swisher, and Paris Gogos. 1999. "PromoCast™: A New Forecasting Method for Promotion Planning." *Marketing Science* 18 (3): 301–316.

Corsten, Daniel, and Thomas Gruen. 2004. "Stock-Outs Cause Walkouts." *Harvard Business Review* 82 (5): 26–28.

Croston, J D. 1972. "Forecasting and Stock Control for Intermittent Demands." *Operational Research Quarterly* 23 (3): 289–303.

D'Aveni, Richard. 2015. "The 3-D Printing Revolution." *Harvard Business Review* 93 (5): 40–48.

Dietvorst, Berkeley J, Joseph P Simmons, and Cade Massey. 2015. "Algorithm Aversion: People Erroneously Avoid Algorithms after Seeing Them Err." *Journal of Experimental Psychology: General* 144 (1): 114–26.

Engle, Robert. 2001. "GARCH 101: The Use of ARCH/GARCH Models in Applied Econometrics." *Journal of Economic Perspectives* 15 (4): 157–68.

Fildes, Robert, Paul Goodwin, Michael Lawrence, and Konstantinos Nikolopoulos. 2009. "Effective Forecasting and Judgmental Adjustments: An Empirical Evaluation and Strategies for Improvement in Supply-Chain Planning." *International Journal of Forecasting* 25 (1): 3–23.

Fildes, Robert, and Fotios Petropoulos. 2015. "Improving Forecast Quality in Practice." *Foresight* 36: 5–12.

Franses, Philip Hans. 2016. "A Note on the Mean Absolute Scaled Error." *International Journal of Forecasting* 32 (1): 20–22.

Gardner, Everette S. 2006. "Exponential Smoothing: The State of the Art—Part II." *International Journal of Forecasting* 22 (4): 637–66.

Gardner, Everette S, and Ed McKenzie. 1985. "Forecasting Trends in Time Series." *Management Science* 31 (10): 1237–46.

Gelper, Sarah, Roland Fried, and Christophe Croux. 2010. "Robust Forecasting with Exponential and Holt–Winters Smoothing." *Journal of Forecasting* 29 (3): 285–300.

Gilliland, Mike. 2013. "FVA: A Reality Check on Forecasting Practices." *Foresight* 29: 14–18.

Goodwin, Paul. 2000. "Correct or Combine? Mechanically Integrating Judgmental Forecasts with Statistical Methods." *International Journal of Forecasting* 16 (2): 261–75.

Goodwin, Paul, and Richard Lawton. 1999. "On the Asymmetry of the Symmetric MAPE." *International Journal of Forecasting* 15 (4): 405–8.

Green, Kesten, and Len Tashman. 2008. "Should We Define Forecast Errors as e = F - A or e = A - F?" *Foresight* 10: 38–40.

———. 2009. "Percentage Error: What Denominator?" *Foresight* 12: 36–40.

Hanley, James A, Lawrence Joseph, Robert W Platt, Moo K Chung, and Patrick Belisle. 2001. "Visualizing the Median as the Minimum-Deviation Location." *The American Statistician* 55 (2): 150–52.

Haran, Uriel, Don A Moore, and Carey K Morewedge. 2010. "A Simple Remedy for Overprecision in Judgment." *Judgment and Decision Making* 5 (7): 467–76.

Harvey, Nigel. 1995. "Why Are Judgments Less Consistent in Less Predictable Task Situations?" *Organizational Behavior and Human Decision Processes* 63 (3): 247–63.

Harvey, Nigel, Teresa Ewart, and Robert West. 1997. "Effects of Data Noise on Statistical Judgement." *Thinking & Reasoning* 3 (2): 111–32.

Hill, Arthur V, Weiyong Zhang, and Gerald F Burch. 2015. "Forecasting the Forecastability Quotient for Inventory Management." *International Journal of Forecasting* 31 (3): 651–63.

Hoover, Jim. 2006. "Measuring Forecast Accuracy: Omissions in Today's Forecasting Engines and Demand-Planning Software." *Foresight* 4: 32–35.

Hyndman, Rob J. 2002. "A State Space Framework for Automatic Forecasting Using Exponential Smoothing Methods." *International Journal of Forecasting* 18 (3): 439–54.

———. 2006. "Another Look at Forecast-Accuracy Metrics for Intermittent Demand." *Foresight* 4: 43–46.

Hyndman, Rob J, Roman A Ahmed, George Athanasopoulos, and Han Lin Shang. 2011. "Optimal Combination Forecasts for Hierarchical Time Series." *Computational Statistics & Data Analysis* 55 (9): 2579–89.

Hyndman, Rob J, and George Athanasopoulos. 2014. "Optimally Reconciling Forecasts in a Hierarchy." *Foresight* 35: 42–44.

Hyndman, Rob J, and Anne B Koehler. 2006. "Another Look at Measures of Forecast Accuracy." *International Journal of Forecasting* 22 (4): 679–88.

Hyndman, Rob J, Anne B Koehler, J Keith Ord, and Ralph D Snyder. 2008. *Forecasting with Exponential Smoothing: The State Space Approach.* Berlin, Germany: Springer.

Hyndman, Rob J, and Andrey V Kostenko. 2007. "Minimum Sample Size Requirements for Seasonal Forecasting Models." *Foresight* 6: 12–15.

Hyndman, Rob J, Alan J Lee, and Earo Wang. 2016. "Fast Computation of Reconciled Forecasts for Hierarchical and Grouped Time Series." *Computational Statistics & Data Analysis* 97: 16–32.

Januschowski, Tim, Stephan Kolassa, Martin Lorenz, and Christian Schwarz. 2013. "Forecasting with In-Memory Technology." *Foresight* 31: 14–20.

Kahneman, Daniel, Dan Lovallo, and Olivier Sibony. 2011. "Before You Make That Big Decision." *Harvard Business Review* 89 (6): 51–60.

Kolassa, Stephan. 2016a. "Evaluating Predictive Count Data Distributions." *International Journal of Forecasting* 32 (3): 788–803.

———. 2016b. "Sometimes It's Better to Be Simple than Correct." *Foresight* 40: 20-26.

Kolassa, Stephan, and Rob J Hyndman. 2010. "Free Open-Source Forecasting Using R." *Foresight* 17: 19-24.

Kolassa, Stephan, and Roland Martin. 2011. "Percentage Errors Can Ruin Your Day (and Rolling Dice Shows How)." *Foresight* 23: 21–29.

Kolassa, Stephan, and Wolfgang Schuetz. 2007. "Advantages of the MAD/Mean Ratio over the MAPE." *Foresight* 6: 40–43.

Kremer, Mirko, Brent Moritz, and Enno Siemsen. 2011. "Demand Forecasting Behavior: System Neglect and Change Detection." *Management Science* 57 (10): 1827–43.

Kremer, Mirko, Enno Siemsen, and Doug Thomas. 2016. "The Sum and Its Parts: Judgmental Hierarchical Forecasting." *Management Science*, Forthcoming.

Kreye, Melanie E, Yee Mey Goh, Linda B Newnes, and Paul Goodwin. 2012. "Approaches to Displaying Information to Assist Decisions under Uncertainty." *Omega* 40 (6): 682–92.

Lapide, Larry. 2014. "S&OP : The Process Revisited." *Journal of Business Forecasting* 34 (3): 12–16.

Larrick, Richard P, and Jack B Soll. 2006. "Intuitions about Combining Opinions: Misappreciation of the Averaging Principle." *Management Science* 52 (1): 111–27.

Lawrence, Michael, Paul Goodwin, and Robert Fildes. 2002. "Influence of User Participation on DSS Use and Decision Accuracy." *Omega* 30 (5): 381–92.

Lawrence, Michael, and Spyros Makridakis. 1989. "Factors Affecting Judgmental Forecasts and Confidence Intervals." *Organizational Behavior and Human Decision Processes* 43 (2): 172–87.

Lawrence, Michael, Marcus O'Connor, and Bob Edmundson. 2000. "A Field Study of Sales Forecasting Accuracy and Processes." *European Journal of Operational Research* 122: 151–60.

Makridakis, Spyros. 1993a. "Accuracy Measures: Theoretical and Practical Concerns." *International Journal of Forecasting* 9 (4): 527–29.

———. 1993b. "The M2-Competition: A Real-Time Judgmentally Based Forecasting Study." *International Journal of Forecasting* 9 (1): 5–22.

Makridakis, Spyros, and Michele Hibon. 2000. "The M3-Competition: Results, Conclusions and Implications." *International Journal of Forecasting* 16 (4): 451–76.

Mannes, Albert E, and Don A Moore. 2013. "A Behavioral Demonstration of Overconfidence in Judgment." *Psychological Science* 24 (7): 1190–97.

Matthews, Robert. 2000. "Storks Deliver Babies (p = 0.008)." *Teaching Statistics* 22 (2): 36–39.

McCarthy, Teresa M, Donna F Davis, Susan L Golicic, and John T Mentzer. 2006. "The Evolution of Sales Forecasting Management: A 20-Year Longitudinal Study of Forecasting Practices." *Journal of Forecasting* 25 (5): 303–24.

Mélard, Guy. 2014. "On the Accuracy of Statistical Procedures in Microsoft Excel 2010." *Computational Statistics* 29: 1095–128.

Mello, John. 2009. "The Impact of Sales Forecast Game Playing on Supply Chains." *Foresight* 13: 13–22.

Miller, Don M, and Dan Williams. 2003. "Shrinkage Estimators of Time Series Seasonal Factors and Their Effect on Forecasting Accuracy." *International Journal of Forecasting* 19 (4): 669–84.

Minnucci, Jay. 2006. "Nano Forecasting: Forecasting Techniques for Short-Time Intervals." *Foresight* 4: 6-10.

Mohammadipour, Maryam, John E Boylan, and Aris A Syntetos. 2015. "The Application of Product-Group Seasonal Indexes to Individual Products." *Foresight* 26: 18–24.

Moritz, Brent, Enno Siemsen, and Mirko Kremer. 2014. "Judgmental Forecasting: Cognitive Reflection and Decision Speed." *Production and Operations Management* 23 (7): 1146–60.

Morlidge, Steve. 2014. "Do Forecasting Methods Reduce Avoidable Error? Evidence from Forecasting Competitions." *Foresight* 32: 34–39.

———. 2015. "Measuring the Quality of Intermittent Demand Forecasts: It's Worse than We've Thought!" *Foresight* 37: 37–42.

Nahmias, Steven. 1994. "Demand Estimation in Lost Sales Inventory Systems." *Naval Research Logistics* 41 (6): 739–57.

Nahmias, Steven, and Tava Olsen. 2015. *Production and Operations Analysis*. 7th edition. Long Grove, IL: Waveland Press.

Oliva, Rogelio, and Noel Watson. 2009. "Managing Functional Biases in Organizational Forecasts: A Case Study of Consensus Forecasting in Supply Chain Planning." *Production and Operations Management* 18 (2): 138–51.

Önkal, Dilek, Paul Goodwin, Mary Thomason, M Sinan Gönül, and Andrew Pollock. 2009. "The Relative Influence of Advice from Human Experts and Statistical Methods on Forecast Adjustments." *Journal of Behavioral Decision Making* 409: 390–409.

Raiffa, Howard. 1968. *Decision Analysis*. Reading, MA: Addison-Wesley.

Richardson, Ronny. 2011. *Business Applications of Multiple Regression*. New York, NY: Business Expert Press.

Rickwalder, Dan. 2006. "Forecasting Weekly Effects of Recurring Irregular Occurences." *Foresight* 4: 16–18.

Robinson, Lynn A. 2006. *Trust Your Gut: How the Power of Intuition Can Grow Your Business*. Chicago, IL: Kaplan Publishing.

Scheele, Lisa M, Marco Slikker, and Ulrich W Thonemann. 2014. "Designing Incentive Systems for Truthful Demand Information Sharing—Theory and Experiment." Working Paper. Cologne, Germany.

Schmidt, Torsten, and Simeon Vosen. 2013. "Forecasting Consumer Purchases Using Google Trends." *Foresight* 30: 38–41.

Schubert, Sean. 2012. "Forecastability: A New Method for Benchmarking and Driving Improvement." *Foresight* 26: 5–13.

Seifert, Matthias, Enno Siemsen, Allègre L Hadida, and Andreas B Eisingerich. 2015. "Effective Judgmental Forecasting in the Context of Fashion Products." *Journal of Operations Management* 36: 33–45.

Shmueli, Galit, and Kenneth C Lichtendahl. 2015. *Practical Time Series Forecasting with R: A Hands-On Guide*. Axelrod Schnall.

Singh, Sujit. 2013. "Supply Chain Forecasting & Planning: Move on from Microsoft Excel?" *Foresight* 31: 6–13.

Smith, Joe. 2009. "The Alignment of People, Process, and Tools." *Foresight* 15: 13–18.

Soyer, Emre, and Robin M. Hogarth. 2012. "The Illusion of Predictability: How Regression Statistics Mislead Experts." *International Journal of Forecasting* 28 (3): 695–711.

Spiegel, Alica. 2014. "So You Think You're Smarter Than A CIA Agent." http://www.npr.org/blogs/parallels/2014/04/02/297839429/-so-you-think-youre-smarter-than-a-cia-agent

Surowiecki, James. 2004. *The Wisdom of Crowds*. New York, NY: Anchor.

Syntetos, Aris A, M Zied Babai, and Everette S Gardner. 2015. "Forecasting Intermittent Inventory Demands: Simple Parametric Methods vs. Bootstrapping." *Journal of Business Research* 68: 1746–52.

Syntetos, Aris A, M Zied Babai, David Lengu, and Nezih Altay. 2011. "Distributional Assumptions for Parametric Forecasting of Intermittent Demand." In *Service Parts Management*, edited by N Altay and L A Litteral, 31–52. London: Springer.

Syntetos, Aris A, and John E Boylan. 2001. "On the Bias of Intermittent Demand Estimates." *International Journal of Production Economics* 71 (1-3): 457–66.

———. 2005. "The Accuracy of Intermittent Demand Estimates." *International Journal of Forecasting* 21 (2): 303–14.

Taylor, P F, and M E Thomas. 1982. "Short Term Forecasting: Horses for Courses." *Journal of the Operational Research Society* 33 (8): 685–94.

Tetlock, Philip, and Dan Gardner. 2015. *Superforecasting*. New York, NY: Crown.

Teunter, Ruud, and Babangida Sani. 2009. "On the Bias of Croston's Forecasting Method." *European Journal of Operational Research* 194 (1): 177–83.

Timme, Stephen G. 2003. "The Real Cost of Holding Inventory." *Supply Chain Management Review* 7 (4): 30–37.

Tonetti, Bill. 2006. "Tips for Forecasting Semi-New Products." *Foresight* 4: 53–56.

Index

OTHER TITLES IN OUR SUPPLY AND OPERATIONS MANAGEMENT COLLECTION

Johnny Rungtusanatham, The Ohio State University
and Joy M. Field, Boston College, *Editors*

- *Better Business Decisions Using Cost Modeling, Second Edition* by Victor Sower and Christopher Sower
- *Improving Business Performance with Lean, Second Edition* by James R. Bradley
- *Lean Communication: Applications for Continuous Process Improvement* by Sam Yankelevitch and Claire F. Kuhl
- *An Introduction to Lean Work Design: Fundamentals of Lean Operations, Volume I* by Lawrence D. Fredendall and Matthieas Thurer
- *An Introduction to Lean Work Design: Standard Practices and Tools of Lean, Volume II* by Lawrence D. Fredendall and Matthias Thurer
- *Leading and Managing Lean* by Gene Fliedner
- *Managing and Improving Quality: Integrating Quality, Statistical Methods and Process Control* by Amar Sahay
- *Mapping Workflows and Managing Knowledge: Using Formal and Tacit Knowledge to Improve Organizational Performance, Volume I* by John Kmetz
- *Mapping Workflows and Managing Knowledge: Dynamic Modeling of Formal and Tacit Knowledge to Improve Organizational Performance, Volume II* by John Kmetz
- *RFID for the Supply Chain and Operations Professional, Second Edition* by Pamela Zelbst and Victor Sower
- *The Unified Theory of Profitability: 25 Ways to Accelerate Growth Through Operational Excellence* by Andrew Miller

Announcing the Business Expert Press Digital Library

Concise e-books business students need for classroom and research

This book can also be purchased in an e-book collection by your library as

- *a one-time purchase,*
- *that is owned forever,*
- *allows for simultaneous readers,*
- *has no restrictions on printing, and*
- *can be downloaded as PDFs from within the library community.*

Our digital library collections are a great solution to beat the rising cost of textbooks. E-books can be loaded into their course management systems or onto students' e-book readers.
The **Business Expert Press** digital libraries are very affordable, with no obligation to buy in future years. For more information, please visit **www.businessexpertpress.com/librarians**.
To set up a trial in the United States, please email **sales@businessexpertpress.com**.

CPSIA information can be obtained
at www.ICGtesting.com
Printed in the USA
FFHW010230030719
53381567-59076FF

9 781606 495025